"Sonia Leung has woven together her ov̶̶̶̶̶̶̶̶̶̶̶̶̶̶̶̶̶̶̶̶̶̶̶̶̶̶̶̶̶̶
and self-discovery as a contemporary Chinese woman from a
background with a story of family history, one that is particular to her
ancestral family's mainland Chinese and overseas Chinese background,
coupled with her parents' decision to move to Hong Kong that proves
significant, sad and transformative for her and her family. This is set
against the recent history of China and Hong Kong. Threaded through
this narrative is Sonia's relation to literature in general and classic Chinese
literature in particular. However, her discovery, as an unhappy and abused
young girl, of popular Taiwan romance novels, is equally as moving. The
self-determination of the protagonists of such novels serves as inspiration
for her to make an extraordinary 'escape' out of Hong Kong. That section
demonstrates, with extraordinary power and poignancy, Sonia's ambition
that is given wings, as it were, by the power of imagination found through
reading." – Xu Xi, author of *That Man in Our Lives*

"When I first read Sonia Leung's work, I was struck by her literary
skills. I was clearly in the hands of a remarkable writer, with a deft hand
for character, imagery, scene. Leung joins to that an unsparing eye for
the tensions of class and gender in contemporary China. Leung is a
remarkably brave narrator, exposing her own abuse, and the trauma of
her family's role in that abuse. In this beautiful read, Leung teaches us
that redemption happens both outside and inside. As #MeToo stalls,
Sonia Leung arrives to show us what that movement really means."

– Susanne Antonetta,
author of *The Terrible Unlikelihood of Our Being Here*

"Leung's writing is punchy and detailed, and there is clearly a very
powerful story of growth and transformation that parallels and throws
light upon China's own journey into the modern world."

– Justin Hill, author of *The Drink and Dream Teahouse*

"One strength Leung decidedly has is a graphic and vivid sense of the physicality of a setting … Related to her graphic and vivid sense of language is the effective use of dialogue, enabling her to quickly bring the reader into the middle of a scene."

— Luis Francia, author of *Eye of the Fish: A Personal Archipelago*

"Sonia Leung's *The Girl Who Dreamed* is an uncompromising and inspiring account of resilience and perseverance in the face of seemingly insurmountable challenges. In a beautifully crafted narrative, rich with allusions to the classics of Chinese literature, Leung details how the life of one girl who dreamed of self-actualisation in Hong Kong was brutally unraveled by those she trusted shortly after rejoining her family in a slum in Diamond Hill. Leung's story – which took 10 years to write – is all the more remarkable considering she took her first English class in Hong Kong aged 12. *The Girl Who Dreamed* marks something of a watershed moment in memoir-writing in Hong Kong literature. Never before have the first-hand experiences of the impoverished mainland immigrants arriving into Hong Kong in the 1980s been so carefully narrated from a girl's and then a young woman's perspective. The narrative of brutal gendered violence experienced at the hands of local and expat men is surely a story that rings true for many women who have migrated to Hong Kong. Leung's memoir gives readers the opportunity to come to terms with the trauma of migration coupled with violence that so many experienced. But her narrative goes further still; in a remarkable display of fortitude and authorial conviction, Leung repeatedly demonstrates how hope can be found in reading and in writing, even when pain becomes too suffocating to endure or even acknowledge."

— Michael O'Sullivan, author of *Lockdown Lovers*

The Girl Who Dreamed

A Hong Kong memoir of triumph against the odds

Sonia Leung

BLACKSMITH BOOKS

The Girl Who Dreamed

ISBN 978-988-76748-5-6

Published by Blacksmith Books
Unit 26, 19/F, Block B, Wah Lok Industrial Centre,
37-41 Shan Mei Street, Fo Tan, Hong Kong
Tel: (+852) 2877 7899
www.blacksmithbooks.com

Copyright © Sonia Leung 2024

Edited by Paul Christensen

The author asserts the moral right to be identified as the author of this work.

All rights reserved. No part of this publication may be reproduced, stored or transmitted in any form or by any means, electronic, mechanical, photocopying, recording or otherwise, without the prior written permission of the publisher.

Contents

Prior Publication Acknowledgments

In earlier versions, the following excerpts have already been published (and some republished) under the same titles (except *Even Butterflies Are Free*, a title made up solely for that excerpt), as follows.

The Moon in a Dog's Eye, *MaLa Literary Journal*, March 2016, Issue 4, and the anthology, *Afterness: Literature from the New Transnational Asia*, 2016, and the online magazine *Chinarrative*, October 2018, Issue 7

Diamond Hill (the second prize winner of Hong Kong's Top Story 2016), *Cha: An Asian Literary Journal*, March 2017, Issue 35, and the anthology on TORCH, University of Oxford, *Personal History of Home,* December 2022

Under the Lychee Trees, *The Shanghai Literary Review*, December 2017, Issue 2

Home of Lost Souls (the third prize winner of Hong Kong's Top Story 2015), *The Shanghai Literary Review*, November 2018, Issue 4, and *West Trestle Review*, July/August 2021

Even Butterflies Are Free, *Remington Review*, Summer 2020

Dai Luk Mui, *Remington Review*, Spring 2021

Author's note

Many of the names in this memoir are pseudonyms.

References to dollars ($) refer to Hong Kong dollars unless otherwise specified; since 1983 one US dollar has been equal to 7.8 Hong Kong dollars.

Foreword

To be asked to write the foreword to such an inspiring and moving memoir is a humbling experience. All the more so, when I realize that I could not understand the language in which many of these events played out. Like something of a mute witness, I read now in English the translation of those brutal episodes from a young migrant girl's life and I ask myself is it more barbaric in English, mindful of all that postcolonialism has taught me about the brutality of the English language. Or, perhaps, giving them to us in English is one way to preserve self in the face of unimaginable pain and loss. When pain becomes so great as to be incomprehensible for a girl, translating it may be all we have to shape it, to give it order. Memoir is after all a deeply personal and revealing genre and one is never sure in engaging with it how much one has to give of oneself.

I met Sonia for the first time on the campus of the Chinese University of Hong Kong. I had invited her to read a piece of her work at a small conference I was organizing on Narrative and Cross-Cultural Humanities for the Department of English in 2018. I wanted the conference to be a mixture of creative and critical work and I had invited Sonia to read in a session called Hong Kong Storytelling. Sonia was the only creative writer who had responded to my request.

Sonia must have felt a little nervous speaking in front of a group that was made up principally of academics. The talks had been good. They were academic papers backed up with well designed PowerPoint presentations. As the organizer, I was doing the job of coming up with appropriate academic questions for each speaker. In other words, events were proceeding in the rather routine manner appropriate to academic conferences. Sonia took to the podium and the mood changed. Something about her words and her way of introducing herself spoke of honesty and of a range of life experiences that had not been touched on yet at the conference. When she began to tell her story everyone listened. No one tried desperately to think of a question. We just listened. We were compelled to listen for Sonia's narrative possessed an authenticity that we had forgotten about. It shattered the academic pretense that had carefully formed about proceedings. I can still recall the silence that greeted Sonia when she finished speaking. I knew that something special had happened and that a pulse of real experience had shone briefly inside the room.

I have kept in touch with Sonia ever since and she has been generous in sharing her work with me. I tried to encourage her to continue with her work whenever I could and a few months after the conference she shared with me a section that now makes up one of the chapters of this book.

Some stories have to be told and Sonia's story is one such story; not only because it is compelling and inspiring and authentic but also because it gives to us in English for the first time an aspect of migrant experience that has not yet appeared in Hong Kong Anglophone literature. Hong Kong literature in English is a vibrant, diverse and vitally important element of Hong Kong culture and of Greater China culture. It is a precious flower; what, in borrowing from Roberto Bolaño, we might call "the magic flower of winter!" Sonia's memoir *The Girl Who Dreamed* nourishes this endangered flower in reminding us of how important survival is. In survival we can discover a reason to persevere that is worth sharing and in the sharing we connect with others who may have experienced similar trauma. Sonia's memoir has the potential then to nourish the genre and also offer healing for those who have been living for so long with similar trauma. In one of her experiences in the memoir she is listening to an unnamed lecturer comparing Li Shangyin and Oscar Wilde on self-sacrifice. Both Li's silkworm and Wilde's nightingale sacrifice themselves for beauty; Sonia shares with these writers in offering us up a vision of beauty as something that is worth the sacrifice. The sacrifice of the artist who takes 10 years to write her story is something that Li and Wilde well understood and it is a tradition that she enriches in the Hong Kong context through her memoir.

Michael O'Sullivan
Former Professor of English,
Chinese University of Hong Kong

Prologue

"Unquiet darkness seized the space, so heavy it could barely leave the ground" – was the atmosphere of the room where Coach raped me that I describe in this memoir. I had the same feeling about Hong Kong in 2022 after yet another return from two and a half years away in Taiwan.

Though I did not leave for political reasons in 2019, it weighed on me. Little did I know how much my city would change. Still, I published my first book, *Don't Cry, Phoenix* – a bilingual (English and Chinese) poetry collection with a CD of ten original songs – in Taiwan in 2020.

Returning, against the flow, to Hong Kong in the spring of 2022, I found the city not just ridden with Covid-19 but also profoundly polarized. I strive to carve a space for myself in Hong Kong's literary land, however feeble and fragile, and endeavor to get my voice heard worldwide.

This memoir tells the stories of my life from birth to the age of twenty-six, which took place in mainland China, Hong Kong, Taiwan, and the United States. I hope the stories resonate with you. In a sense, the memoir is not really about me, but rather, through my eyes, I let you into my world, and as a result of reading, it may enlarge yours.

As a memoirist, I believe in the transformative power of life stories to bring people together, expand our cognitive horizons, and gently unlock our true potential for empathy and wisdom.

Part One: Broken

Hong Kong

1986 – 1989

Diamond Hill

I crossed the border and entered Hong Kong when I was twelve in June 1986.

Escorted by an uncle from my father Leung's clan, my younger sister and I took the overnight bus from Nan'an county in China's Fujian province to Shenzhen.

We then passed through Lo Wu Control Point and embarked on a Kowloon-bound train to reunite with our parents, elder sister, and elder brother, who had come to Hong Kong two and a half years earlier.

Uncle Leung led us off at the Diamond Hill station. When we reached the street level, the view in front stung me – low, gray, sheet-metal huts stuck together eerily, like something out of a war movie back in the fifties.

How could this be Hong Kong, every Mainlander's dreamland?

Maybe my eyes were playing tricks on me.

Gloomy eateries and rickety stalls, mostly operated by older women, sold clothes, cooking utensils, condiments, meat, fruit, and vegetables. And then there was a "playground" – an irregular-shaped space with an old, bumpy, concrete table-tennis table. That was all.

We headed into a labyrinth of dark, narrow, winding alleys. Once inside the maze with the huts closing in and the sewage running in half-open drains next to the paths, the smell hit me. The stench was dense, like a tangible line in space. The reek of urine, feces, sour cockroaches, and rotten rats made up its density. It was useless to breathe carefully.

The smell was pungent and thick; it replaced the air. A hot substitute filled my lungs, seeped into my blood, and made me its creature. Once

I took a deep breath, I was no longer an air breather. I metamorphosed into another species.

Hong Kong was a British territory then, and the government did not recognize my father's doctor credentials or my mother's teacher credentials from China. My parents knew about this but still chose to come. It was mainly due to economic considerations.

China was going through an enormous economic reform. My parents' salary in their respective government positions was much less than that of my uncles, who started their own businesses. And then, there was this problem of our whole family getting stuck in Datian ["big rice paddy"], an impoverished, mountainous county, where our *hukou* [household register] would permanently constrain us.

Going to Hong Kong was a rare chance for my family to flee from those unfavorable conditions, our golden way out. And unlike the commercial world, once you relinquished your job with the government, you could not request to have it back or reapply for it.

There could be no return for my parents.

They became factory workers in Hong Kong.

The monthly salary each earned as a teacher and a doctor in China was RMB45.50 (about US$5), whereas a factory worker in Hong Kong made about $2,500 (US$320) monthly. The cost of living differed tremendously between the two places, with Hong Kong on the much higher side. Still, the surplus was significant.

The economic gain in Hong Kong helped my parents compensate for losing their high social status. With the financial superiority, my parents could return to their hometown, Nan'an, during Chinese New Year with grace and glory, knowing they still held the lead over their younger siblings.

During those visits, my parents would wear their most expensive clothes and shoes and act like they had an abundant life in Hong Kong. And that mattered to them tremendously – having face in front of relatives.

After my parents and two elder siblings arrived in Hong Kong on the last day of 1983, they squeezed into the room my fifth uncle rented. Fifth Uncle came a year before them. He shared another room there with a man from our village. At that time, mainly single men came to Hong Kong, working to send money home.

My parents later found a rooftop room in Ngau Tau Kok, near their Kwun Tong factory, and set up home there. After they applied for my younger sister and me to join them, they began to save every penny possible.

About a year later, one day they heard a young couple from Leung's clan was getting a divorce and was eager to sell their hut in Diamond Hill. Uncle Chan, a relative from my mother's side, an "old Hong Konger," and a Chinese medicine man with an established home practice, carried an air of superiority and went with my parents to "talk price" or bargain with the young couple.

Uncle Chan got the price down from $60,000 to $48,000, and he had them agree, reluctantly, to accept half of that price first and the rest six months later.

Mother was earning about $3,000 a month, working from 7am to 3pm, six days a week, and went to the market daily to get fresh food as they did not yet have a refrigerator. She also cooked and took care of all the housework.

Father was earning about $4,000 a month. After working the full-time seven-to-three shift he then added overtime every day until 7pm.

After one year, they had saved about $4,000. To meet the half payment of $24,000, they borrowed $10,000 from each of Uncle Chan and Uncle Li, my father's brother-in-law, who owned a furniture shop, and paid the couple. Then, for the next six months, both of them worked from 7am to 7pm, and Father would stay on and work until 9pm if such work was available.

They saved and borrowed some more and paid the rest off on time. The contract of ownership was a thin piece of paper. Nobody remembered what was written on it and which authority, if any, approved and issued it. There were no chops on it.

They moved into Diamond Hill in the spring of 1986, half a year before our arrival.

The hut was only a half-hut. Like a jigsaw puzzle, our lower half and another upper one made a full hut. A rusty iron gate with peeling claret paint on the ground floor served as our entry.

When you opened the gate, two steps led you down to the only room. Its contents included two tarnished iron bunk beds, one of which was double width, a light brown wooden closet, a gloomy-looking bedside table with a mirror on top, and an old, bulky TV set. My parents bought these second-hand from either Leung or Chan's clans.

Between the furniture, we had a square in the middle; its extent equal to a person with out-stretched arms. This remaining center was our living and dining area. We dined with a folding table and put it away after each meal. One or two would sit close to the closet watching TV. For our homework or reading, we did it in our beds.

Also located inside the room, another set of two steps led to a dark corner to the left side of the gate. The corner was beneath a steep staircase of the other half-hut owner, another family. They lived right above us. But they had a separate entry where a different door opened onto the stairs that led up to their room.

We used the small, dim corner underneath this staircase as our kitchen and bathroom – a narrow strip with a squat toilet; we stood on its sides to shower.

At first, I liked the coziness of the hut. The two-and-a-half-year separation from my family made the initial reunion thrilling. And it felt safe to be so close to them. Perhaps we had arrived at our Promised Land, were united at last, and could live happily ever after.

So I dreamed.

But once the effect of the reunion excitement wore off, the reality set in. The bubble of my dream soon burst.

My parents continued to work long hours to support the expanded family. Elder Sister and Brother found summertime jobs and worked most of the time. They locked Younger Sister and me inside the hut, where we watched TV all day.

I was the least favorite child in my family. Being a dark-skinned, super sensitive, and most father-like daughter, I was "the nail in my mother's eye," as a Chinese saying goes, meaning I could easily irritate her.

My mother had a disastrous relationship with my father. And the stress she had from living in Hong Kong as a marginal person and the burden she carried by raising a relatively big family in this expensive city added massive weight to her shoulders. She became short-tempered, and I often got in her way.

One day, my mother came home from work around 7:30pm and began cooking.

I did homework in my single upper bunk. Brother watched TV from his lower one, and Mother started talking to him.

"You know, son, they think I'm stupid."

"Er, why?"

I barely heard Brother's mumbling over the background noise of the TV. So I strained my ears to catch what they were saying.

"This morning, our assembly line's leader asked me if I knew how to write my name!"

She sounded like she was about to cry.

"If they only knew – I was a teacher who taught Chinese to hundreds of students!"

She started crying. I could sense it.

Kuang. Kuang. The noises of the spatula striking the wok called out to me.

I hurried down from my bunk and asked:

"*Ma*, are you okay? Can I help you with anything?"

"You, go away!"

She brandished the spatula and shouted.

I froze.

Brother gave me a quick look and a smirk.

He walked toward the narrow kitchen, looking at Mother on the second step. There was no space for him to go in. He stretched his hand, reached out to the dish on the stove, picked up a slice of pork, and slid it into his mouth.

I drooled.

Mother breathed and sighed deeply.

"Oh, my son, you must be starving now. I'll finish cooking soon."

They carried on with the small talk.

I became non-existent to them. If I could vanish into the air, I would not feel so empty and hungry for food, attention, validation, and love.

I pressed my lips together and shut my eyes for a long minute to prevent tears from coming out. But they stung behind my eyelids and triggered a hard, painful lump in my throat.

A sense of worthlessness gathered its power and seized my stomach. It hastened into my lungs and heart, ran further up to my brain, and embedded itself there for good. I wanted to shake it off and scream. But I found neither the nerve nor the energy to do so.

My stomach snarled and howled before. Now, it was silent. Only pains persisted. And it felt like a part of me was dissipating.

Maybe I would become non-existent in this place called home.

Father's defense mechanism for life was to retreat into himself.

He avoided work-related talk. At home, he hardly spoke but only shouted when he got drunk. Like an unexploded bomb, he could go off anytime. When Father came home at about 9:30pm from overtime, he would eat and wash it down with a beer, followed by *Kaoliang* [sorghum liquor] or whisky, totally lost in his own world.

Usually, I stayed in my upper bunk and suppressed my urge to go to the toilet. Visiting the bathroom meant that I must squeeze past the table's edge where Father was sitting. The attention I would attract terrified me. But the more I suppressed the urge, the more urgent and frequent it became.

I despised myself.

If Father came home earlier, he would have dinner with us in silence and finish his meal quickly. He took a shower, and when he came out, we gobbled down the food and put away the table and chairs. Father sat on the edge of his lower double bunk, putting his feet on the bedside chair, and flipped through the newspaper.

After a while, Father pushed the paper away and moved into the darker, inner part of the bed. He lay propped against his pillow and watched TV. The sound of his light snorts would soon follow.

During his weekly day off, he often visited the cinema. He would buy a $10 ticket that allowed him to watch movies all day.

The films ranged from detective to pornography, from western to eastern. It did not matter. So long as it kept him away from reality – his unrequited love for my mother, his denigrating factory work, his family burdens – he welcomed it. And that was what he did on his days off, week after week, month after month, spending all day alone inside a dark cinema watching movies.

Later, when he discovered the excitement of horse racing, he started close-reading the newspaper's racing section. He studied the horses like he studied the characters in Russian novels when he was young. He kept sharp pencils by the bedside table and made enthusiastic, extensive notes on the paper about the horses, their conditions, and winning and losing records. His scribbles reminded me of the comments he wrote in his diary after reading the novels. Except now, the scribbles were figures. He gave up on words, forgoing his intellectual self.

Father became an excessive smoker, drinker, and gambler. When he gambled, he second-guessed himself. Father bet on many different horses in one race and often lost. And he lost big. When he won, he won small because of his thin betting. But like many gamblers, the insubstantial winning was enough to keep my father going.

Father was very proud of his winnings. When he won, he would come home smiling. Since this rarely happened, I felt awkward when he smiled. I was unsure whether I should smile with him or rather weep with joy because, finally, something made my father happy.

On the special occasions of his winnings, Father might bring home a white plastic bag with a polystyrene box that carried *siu-mei*. *Siu-mei* [Cantonese barbecue meat] can be *char-siu*, the sticky, crimson barbecue pork; *siu-yuk*, the crispy skin, succulent roasted pork; *siu-ngo* or *siu-aap*, the rich, flavorful, juicy roasted goose or duck.

If Father won a bit more than usual in late autumn, he might come home carrying a large black plastic bag with the fresh Shanghai hairy crabs. He was very pleased with himself and liked to share by *ga-sung* [adding a dish] to our dinner.

On an early winter evening, I was in my bunk reading. Elder Sister and Younger Sister were in their upper double bunk doing homework.

Brother sat in the living area playing on his Game Boy.

Guang. Father pulled open the tarnished iron gate and sprinted down the steps, almost leaping into the room. In an uncharacteristically high-pitched voice, he said to Mother:

"Wingwai, look what I've bought for us all. It's the sweet, tasty crab! Such gourmet food. We can all enjoy it tonight!"

Like a little boy, he raised a bag of live crabs high (I could hear their claws' slow, vague wavering inside the bag). Father had a broad grin on his face. His eyes were twinkling, eagerly anticipating Mother's praise.

Neither giving the slightest glimpse at him nor the bag of crabs, she replied:

"Yeah, it's your favorite food. You're sure to have a fine feast."

Her words might as well have been a bucket of ice water poured violently over him.

Father's face turned pale.

He froze for a moment or two.

Then he ascended one step toward the kitchen, chucking the bag of expensive crabs into the small sink next to Mother's left elbow. He put down his other gear, took out a pack of Marlboro Red and a lighter, and headed back out the gate.

Once he disappeared behind the door, Mother gave an exaggerated, loud sigh. She then winked at Brother and signaled him to come closer to her. In a quiet and scornful voice, she said:

"Oh, your father is such a cranky creature! I can't even joke with him a little!"

Haha, she and Brother shared a short, derisive laugh.

My sisters must have had their earplugs in, for they were undisturbed.

I rushed down, pretending to look for something inside the closet. But I raised my head and gazed out of the gate.

Father's shoulders were heaving in anguish. He faced a malodorous drainage ditch and dragged on his cigarette.

He had no place to go, no one to share with. I would not talk to anyone, either.

He did not drink outside because he did not want to get drunk and become a laughing stock to the Hongkongers who already looked down on him, the Mainlander.

The social hierarchy of Hong Kong at that time looked roughly like this: the white Europeans sat atop the pyramid, then mixed-race Eurasians, followed by early Guangdong immigrants' descendants in the middle, and finally new immigrants, especially those from other provinces of China like us, together with the Filipinos, Indians, Pakistanis, and Africans at the base.

Father finished his cigarette and immediately started another one. His shoulders stopped heaving. He put his left hand into his trouser pocket and leaned slightly on the edge of a cracking gray wall next to the drainage ditch.

The wall's grayness had primarily turned into dirty black; damp, green mold grew everywhere. The height of the wall was only up to Father's shoulders. Suddenly, it looked like he did not know where to put his head or what to do with it. He tilted it to the left and then right and then left again.

I wanted to sit on top of that wall and let my lap pillow his head.

Instead, I turned and clambered back up to my bunk. I could not let Mother or Brother see the tears in my eyes. They would count me as Father's ally and alienate me further. It was terrifying. I kept my face toward the wall and my back toward Father, hoping for his forgiveness.

Like a tiny frog in a deep well, I could only see a small portion of the Hong Kong sky.

During that first summer of arrival, the only time I traveled out of Diamond Hill was with Elder Sister and Younger Sister. To celebrate our reunion, Elder Sister took half a day off work, took us out, and treated us to lunch.

She took us to the McDonald's in Yue Man Square, close to her summer job in the same factory as my parents in Kwun Tong.

As it was my first time dining out in Hong Kong, I got so excited I could not sleep the night before. When I entered McDonald's, it felt like a historical moment. The warm and distinctive smell of the food, the beautifully dressed children and their parents, and the loud and intriguing Cantonese language absorbed me. I lost myself in this fabulous fairyland.

Elder Sister tugged at my sleeve and brought me back to reality. She found a table and taught Younger Sister and me our first Cantonese phrase: *jau jan*, "there are people," or in this case, "the table is taken." After she ensured I pronounced it correctly, she went to buy food and drinks for us.

For the next fifteen minutes, I kept saying *jau jan*, *jau jan* to whoever passed by and glanced at our table. It felt incredible: I was doing an excellent job of watching over my younger sister in this alien public place and protecting our table simultaneously.

But then, when a mother and a daughter passed by, I repeated the exact phrase. She uttered so many words and so fast it felt like a burst of cannon fire.

I got my first taste of Cantonese – rough, aggressive, and piercing. Fujianese and Mandarin sounded smoother and gentler. A kind of homesickness I did not know then stole over me, weighing me down. I forgot what I ate afterward.

However, how I felt when I came out of McDonald's stayed in my mind. It was as if I had stepped across another major threshold of my life. Now that I had eaten American food, for some reason, I believed I could go to America, too.

It was at that moment that I vaguely understood why my parents left behind their prestigious jobs and endured all the difficulties to bring us, their four children, here. They wanted us to have a bigger world, a bigger dream.

We took the bus home. It was also the first ride in a double-deck bus for Younger Sister and me. My heart was thumping as we ascended the spiral stairs to the upper deck.

Younger Sister ran to the front left seat; Elder Sister followed suit and sat beside her. I took the one directly across the aisle. We chatted away merrily, marveling at the city scenery.

I stole a glance at Elder Sister, a familiar stranger. At sixteen, she looked so grown and elegant, like a fully-fledged swan. Younger Sister, at ten, still had not lost her baby fat, like a cute and chubby duckling snuggling up to her striking sister.

I smiled to myself. Even if I would always be an ugly duckling next to my sweet sisters, I did not mind as long as they included me. I was thrilled and grateful that I could go out with them and enjoy this sisterly trip.

During the ride, Elder Sister told us that Kwun Tong and Diamond Hill were in Kowloon East. Kowloon West and South had places like Tsim

Sha Tsui and Jordan (such exotic names) full of tourists and shoppers, bustling with noise and excitement.

Elder Sister visited those areas once with friends before her summer job started.

I looked at her with new admiration, dreaming about when I would visit those places.

She also explained what the peninsula meant and told us about the New Territories, north of Kowloon, up to the Lo Wu border, where we had crossed, and also encompassing outlying islands.

Then, there was Hong Kong Island.

I could not believe my ears. The size and diversity of Hong Kong amazed me.

Knowing that there was an actual place called Hong Kong Island and that the *Wai do lei aa gong*, or Victoria Harbour, separated it from us, the "Kowlooners," I felt another voyage or challenge lay ahead, waiting for me to conquer it before I could truly arrive in Hong Kong.

Dai Luk Mui

Instead of a tiger, I became a rabbit in Hong Kong.

There was an age discrimination law in Hong Kong back then. Primary school graduates over fourteen would automatically be disqualified from applying for a premier secondary school, no matter how good their grades were. The law was because many mainland Chinese child immigrants like my siblings and I had to resume our studies in a lower class to catch up on our English. At that time in the Mainland, English only started in secondary school. And because we were older, the government assumed we had an advantage over the local students on topics other than English. So, the government implemented such a law to try to counter the assumed unfairness.

My elder sister and brother suffered from this age discrimination law and got into undesired secondary schools. My parents did not want the law to hurt my younger sister and me. So they reduced our ages by a year on our immigration application form. In those days, there was no birth certificate in mainland China. The application form was the basis of our identification in Hong Kong. Instead of 1974, the tiger year, my Hong Kong passport and identification card now state that 1975, the year of the rabbit, was my birth year. But then, the government abolished this law before my primary school graduation. It was an unnecessary change on my part.

I should feel happy that I gained a year on paper. But it was not the case. This birth year change in my Hong Kong identification documents left me feeling like an impostor – someone with a borrowed identity who could never be her authentic self again.

In the second half of August 1986, my younger sister and I took a few entrance exams for nearby primary schools. Eventually, a small Christian primary school's afternoon section accepted us. Its morning section belonged to the mainstream, regular local students. As expected, we were down two grades to catch up on our English.

The school was by a hillside next to a government housing estate. When school began on 1 September that year, I could understand and speak some Cantonese. On 2 September 1986, I had my first English lesson.

The school bell rang. A tall, angular woman walked in. She had short, curly hair and wore oval-shaped glasses with silver-colored frames. Her broad shoulders and straight back made her look even taller. She carried a stack of books in her left arm, a square box like a shoulder bag on her right, and an aura of authority.

The students stood up at first sight of her and chanted:

"Good afternoon, Miss..."

I quickly rose but did not know how to recite the greeting.

"Good afternoon, class."

Miss's voice was thin but firm. She put down her books on the teaching table.

Then she took out a small microphone attached to the black box. It was my first time seeing a portable amplifier. *Whirr. Whirr.* She adjusted the volume of the speaker.

"We will take attendance now," she said in Cantonese.

Her voice came through the amplifier, sounding distant and surreal.

It made me feel like I was suddenly being thrown into one of those sci-fi TV shows and becoming a part of it. My brother loved those shows, but I found no fun in them.

"Angkie Chan," Miss called.

"Present," someone replied.

One after another, it went on.

"Fongling Leung."

"Fongling?"

Miss looked around and fixed her eyes on me. In Cantonese, she asked why I did not reply to her.

I understood what she said but did not know or was too afraid to utter a word. My legs shook, and my teeth chattered. An urge to pee struck me. I quickly tightened my buttocks. But the more I tried to be calm, the more distressed I became.

Desperately, I opened my mouth to answer, but it remained a small vacant "o."

My mind went blank. No words would come out.

Miss signaled me to go to the blackboard and write my name on it.

Knowing that I could not avoid it, I dragged myself up there. I stood before the board, facing the unknown – not knowing how to spell my name. I had not learned my ABCs yet.

Giggles began breaking out. As I remained frozen, laughter pealed across the classroom.

I felt naked, stupid – a plucked rabbit.

Finally, I was allowed to return to my seat. As I walked back, I struggled to stop myself from trembling. The stares came flooding in from all directions, and they threatened to drown me. I sat low but kept afloat, setting my imagination free.

A mosquito net started spreading itself around me. I breathed. But then, I soon discovered that the real mosquitoes were not outside; they were the thoughts inside my head that often launched their attacks.

After that first English lesson, my classmates called me *Dai Luk Mui*.

The name implied that I was a stupid Mainland girl. It encapsulated my appearance well, though, because my dark skin was peasant-like, my lips took on a matte, bruised purple hue, and my relatively big eyes were dusky – they swarmed with brooding melancholy and so much fear and loss. The wickedest thing was my bowl-cut hair, which looked like an upside-down wok dangling over my head.

During recess, I strolled alone around the periphery of the outdoor basketball court.

"*Dai Luk Mui.*"

"Oh, look, the *Dai Luk Mui* is coming!"

Some boys and girls pointed at me. They yelled and laughed when I passed by.

As if my body stank (maybe I did suck up the stench of my slum), they never came too close. Instead, they ran around me and encircled me like an unloved cat with an injured limb. They poked at the cat's wound and had immense fun teasing the poor creature.

The fable of the Moon rabbit rushed to my mind. I had heard the parable when I was about five on a Moon Festival night back in China's Jiyang township, where I was born. Closing my eyes, I imagined myself as the rabbit that jumped into the fire and sacrificed itself to be the food offered to the bodhisattva.

Maybe I was in that fire now, sacrificing myself for a good cause. But what was it? And why? *Hahaha.* The classmates' shrill laughter pulled me back to reality.

Some skipping girls stopped and looked in my direction. One or two tittered.

Some boys sat on the benches reading comic books, raised their heads, and gave me sympathetic looks. Just as quickly, some looked down at their books, and others turned around to start hasty conversations.

I threw back my head to prevent tears from falling.

School used to be heaven to me. In Jiyang, where my mother was a teacher, and in Nan'an, when my younger sister and I stayed behind, I had been a starlet elementary six student with many followers. But now, my classmates looked down on me like a filthy stray cat.

No, I would not cry in front of them. But tears kept coming. I held my head high, wiping them away with the back of my hand. Since the early afternoon, the wind had gathered speed; its moaning sounded soothing. The bare and gravelly hill backdropped the basketball court with its thick chain-link fence. Despite my raised gaze, I could not see much beyond the present.

One day, I discovered a book corner.

The area was a few doors from the teachers' office on the second floor. Colorful children's storybooks in Chinese and English stood side-by-side on the two bookshelves.

The book corner became my place of refuge.

I devoured *Alice's Adventures in Wonderland*, *Little Women*, and *Grimm's Fairy Tales*. My favorite was *The Secret Garden*. One minute, I identified with the lonely Mary, angry and anxious; the next, I assumed the role of Dickon, a good-natured boy who could communicate with animals. But then, Colin's cries crept into my head, where his pain and hopelessness met mine. In the end, I entered the secret garden with Mary, Dickon, and Colin. Together, we thrived.

I read the bilingual version of these books and copied the vocabulary I found there into my notebooks. I made sentences out of these new words to memorize them better and faster. When I wrote a good English sentence that sounded musical when reciting it, my heart fluttered with triumph.

Through these active reading and writing practices, I regained some confidence and began believing I could find my way back to the forest and reclaim my tiger self again.

Ping Pong

I was thirteen, and my English had improved.

By the second half of Primary 5, I became one of the top three students out of all grade five classes, including the morning and afternoon schools.

My classmates ceased to call me *Dai Luk Mui*. Instead, they came close to me and asked me about my study methods. They also inquired about the materials that I focused on reviewing before exams.

Acting friendly, I hung around with them, joked with them, and answered their questions. But whenever a chance came, I would quickly escape to my place of sanctuary, the book corner. Not once did I invite any of my classmates there.

One day, returning home from school, I passed the "playground" area in our slum with its old, bumpy, concrete table-tennis table. As usual, some boys were playing and hanging around there. For some reason, on that particular day, I stopped by the roadside and looked on.

Even the best of them was not much of a player. The ball hardly bounced on the table. They sent it flying all the time.

I thought I could do better than that (though I had no idea where I had gotten such confidence from). Soon after having such a thought, I ran home, changed into shorts, and ran back out again.

I walked toward the table and asked the boys if they would let me play with them. They were reluctant. So I made them an offer: I would run and help them pick up balls ten times before playing. They agreed since they chased and picked up balls more often than hitting them.

Finally, it was my turn.

A boy stepped aside and lent me his paddle.

When I gripped the paddle's handle, it felt great between my thumb and second finger. It gave me a sense of control, a power over something. I was spellbound and never wanted to let the paddle go again.

Ping, the sound of the ball bouncing on the table; *Pong*, the tune of the paddle touching the ball – these two musical notes connected with my heartstrings. They enchanted me no end.

Every cell in my body came alive when I played and made the ping pong sounds with the solid paddle in my grip.

Playing ping pong made me feel like a person again for the first time since I had come to live in this squatter village. When I played, even the rotten stench of the shantytown ceased to bother me.

Saving up my pocket money, I bought myself a simple penhold paddle. Its rubber was thin, and its wood was coarse and heavy. But it was an absolute treasure to me.

I played the game almost every day after school with the boys. After a while, they welcomed me and even let me jump the queue sometimes because I was upbeat and helpful. I always picked up balls for them when it was not my turn.

When I played, I laughed a lot. My body felt lighter – an endless supply of energy kept pumping in. It was surprising to discover that I possessed this sunny, boyish quality.

This new, sporty, and merry me echoed Baochai, one of the three protagonists of Cao Xueqin's *Dream of the Red Chamber*.

Dream, my favorite Chinese novel, is one of China's Four Great Classical Novels, emerging episodically in the mid-18th century during the Qing dynasty. I read a simplified version when I was ten.

In an early scene, Baochai appeared in the Grand View Garden corner, jumping up a few times to catch butterflies. She always paid attention to things above her, in the heavens, whereas Daiyu, her cousin and another protagonist, often looked downwards to the ground, noticing the fallen petals.

Baochai came from a wealthy and prominent family with a royal background. Her father died when she was young, and her older brother,

Pan, was a rake. To protect the family name and fortune, Baochai became unusually precocious. At about fourteen, she took charge of the family's diversified businesses, managing them behind the scenes.

Baochai grew into a forward-thinking lady with a "round" personality. She was a sophisticated people-pleaser who often said what others wanted to hear and acted cautiously to avoid offending anyone. Aspiring to be the emperor's concubine, Baochai patiently awaited her turn. She believed the palace was her future home, where she belonged.

Baochai's third cousin, Baoyu, is the main character; the book is essentially his story. We learn that Baoyu loved and cared about Baochai and Daiyu because they were both beautiful and talented.

Dream detailed these three's teenage years, retracing their personal development through life events and their poetry.

In Baoyu's eye, Baochai personified the spring because she was healthy, sensible, and assertive. But she could be pretentious, pragmatic, and calculating, too.

Daiyu, on the other hand, embodied the autumn because she was fragile, sensitive, and insecure but also intelligent, creative, original, and candid.

Both Baochai and Daiyu existed in me – how thrilling.

A boy from the playground of our slum who played table tennis with me often mentioned a youth recreational center. It was close to the school where I was studying. So I asked him more.

The boy told me that the center had two excellent table-tennis tables. He said he was reluctant to go and play there because the players were more skillful and from the housing estate around the center – a tight group. He did not want to stand out and look silly. So he gave up the chance to play there.

But that was not me. The prospect of engaging in an ideal environment with advanced players excited me. I decided to go there the next day after school to check it out.

The Baochai in me took over. Just like her, I was eager to explore. Eager to evolve. Keen to get to a better place. Bettering myself. Always.

I found the youth center on the ground floor of the housing estate. The minute I entered, the sacred sounds of *ping pong* and the kids' laughter greeted me. I leaned in but could not see them playing from the doorway.

So I approached the reception area and asked to join in. The procedure turned out to be relatively easy – I filled in a form with elementary information and got a temporary member's card straight away. It granted me immediate access. I was in, just like that. How awesome.

And it felt like an exciting, fresh chapter of my life opening right in front of my bewildered wide-open eyes.

I hurried through a narrow corridor with a small office by its side and reached the common area for games, TV watching, and conversation. Then I rushed forward and arrived at the door of the first table-tennis room.

The authentic, professional table-tennis table enthralled me. It looked grand yet compact and slim, and its inky green surface appeared velvety and regal. I had an impulse to open my arms and lay my cheek on the table's silken top. But I quickly eliminated such an inane instinct – I could not afford to make a fool of myself so soon.

Acting cool and calm, I looked on.

About fifteen boys were there. They did play better than the boys in my slum, and their paddles looked finer too. There was an inner room with some more boys playing whose voices sounded deeper.

But I did not want to look in there yet. I might be intimidated and chicken out as a result. For now, I fixed my gaze gladly on the rich green table in front of me and dreamed about playing my heart out.

The next day, I plucked up the courage and joined the queue to play.

As the boys lived in the housing estate around the center, I was an outsider and the only girl player. So, I kept quiet and tried to blend in. Being short-haired, skinny, and boyish-looking, they seemed to pay no attention to me.

After a while, I also stopped feeling self-conscious around them. We played amicably together for three or four hours almost every day after school. But I kept my distance from the inner table. It belonged to the much more skilled players, and I was not one of them yet.

I determined to get myself there soon – how wondrous to see where you could go next.

After a few months, it became apparent that a tall, rangy young man controlled the inner, superior room. He was about fifteen or sixteen. Everyone called him Wongji [Prince]. Seriously.

Wongji was not distinctively handsome – a pale complexion and an expressionless face. But when he played, he radiated self-confidence and tremendous charm. And then his eyes – big and beautiful – shimmered in the light of the fluorescent tube.

Wongji's agile and graceful moves reflected his lean and fit body very well.

When Wongji served, he set the ball spinning in many ways – back, top, side, cork – his opponent had difficulty returning. As an offensive-style player, he frequently played powerful strokes including the hit, loop, counter-hit, flick, and smash.

He carried out all the actions to perfection, according to my admiring eye, of course.

Soon, I found myself becoming an offensive-style player. It matched the tiger in me. But the new rabbit in me craved safety. So I acquired the defensive strokes – push, chop, block, lob – and tried to master these moves. Also, I adopted the more versatile shake-hand-grip style.

After spending multiple hours daily playing in the center after school, I frequented Ngau Chi Wan public library to find table-tennis training guides.

An unquenchable thirst for becoming a great player propelled me to action. Closely studying the books and zealously practicing the moves mentioned inside became my regular rituals. Furthermore, I followed the guides' advice and began building my muscles. Adopting a routine for deep stretching, I was also developing the flexibility of a player's body.

About half a year later, I kept winning.

The playmates cast laudatory looks on me whenever I played. It felt like when my beloved Teacher Li, back in Nan'an, read my compositions aloud in front of our class, which he often did. The sense of triumph was revived from deep within.

Amidst all these advances, I caught fleeting glimpses of Wongji.

Whenever he passed by, I could feel his slowing steps and the slight shifts of his body toward my direction.

I was afraid to catch his eye, fearing it was only my imagination. But he did pass by much more frequently these days. Lately, he had paused long enough for me to register his presence and attention before he walked on.

Wongji's precious glimpses, brief visits, and nods were a bridge, albeit surrounded by the fog of uncertainty, for me to cross from the old world where I felt ugly and unlovable to a hopeful new place.

Wongji, six other talented and enthusiastic boys, and I impressed the center's manager. He organized us into a team and aimed for us to enter competitions on behalf of the center.

We welcomed the idea by practicing harder; the manager went further and recruited a coach to lead and train us.

On the late afternoon of a splendid spring day, a man came and stood alone close to the door between the two table-tennis rooms.

He might be a new staff member. Because if he were the coach, the manager would surely make a proper introduction or at least be there accompanying the man. So, I stopped paying attention to him but threw myself into my play.

It was my lucky day; I stroked superbly. After a few rounds, I suddenly realized the man still stood there, observing me or us playing the entire time.

I blushed, feeling a bit uneasy.

The manager appeared and asked us to stop.

He told the non-selected boys that the tables were reserved for the newly established team to conduct training and politely asked them to leave.

Out of nearly thirty, only eight of us could stay. When I looked at the boys' defeated backs, I prided myself on being a chosen one.

The manager stood next to the man and told us he was our new coach and would train us twice a week. The manager continued to brief us on the upcoming plans.

Taking the opportunity, I observed Coach closer.

The first thing that struck me was the elegiac element in his eyes. He reminded me of my father, a younger version of my father, perhaps in his thirties. His eyes were smaller. But my father's eyes shrank over the years, or maybe it was the effect of the heavy, thick, black-framed glasses that he wore.

But the melancholy in my father's eyes stayed vividly in my mind. Coach's eyes mirrored that element as he gazed at the table's legs and looked as if he was engaged in deep thought. His air of being alone in a crowd was a quality my father possessed.

Then I realized both had similar tousled hair, though Coach's looked more like it was permed, unlike my father's natural curl.

When the manager finished his briefing, he shook hands with the coach and left us.

Coach asked the eight of us to circle him. We did as told, except for Wongji.

Wongji stepped back and perched on a table's edge. With his arms folded across his chest, he looked on as if from somewhere afar. His passion and involvement in forming this team seemed to have dissipated. His face became one of a poker player.

Coach gave us an introduction to his training style and a program rundown. He then went on to tell us about the competitions we could enter.

He turned to me and asked my name.

Startled, I failed to respond.

A boy shouted out my name:

"Fongling! Coach, her name is Fongling."

"Well, Fongling, please step into the middle."

I stood transfixed, wondering why.

"Come. You guys know that I have watched you all play since I arrived. Fongling, you impressed me the most."

Tilting my lowered head slightly, I glimpsed Wongji.

He sat up a little and looked in my direction.

I diverted my gaze, but not quickly enough.

As everyone was waiting, I dragged myself and moved into the circle.

Once I got there, Coach exclaimed:

"Well done, Fongling!"

Then he gave my back a pat of encouragement.

My muscles relaxed a bit. I smiled back at Coach.

He turned to his bag and took out a table-tennis paddle.

"Fongling, this is a paddle I used and won many games."

He looked me in the eyes and went on:

"I would like to pass it on to you as a present. I know you will represent our team well and win many games. Come, accept this honor, and do us proud!"

Fully flattered, I was too flabbergasted to make a sound.

Coach's passion pumped up the atmosphere of that small table tennis room and our circle. High-spiritedly, my teammates hooted and cheered.

An exquisite Butterfly paddle, the world's leading table tennis brand, was waiting for me to accept. I could not believe my luck and remained motionless.

Coach stepped closer. Leaning forward, he came face to face with me.

His cologne smelled like a light sea breeze, much subtler than his passion.

With the calming effect of his scent, he reached out his hand and took up mine. Gently but firmly, he placed the paddle in my palm.

The exceptionally smooth, light, but stiff Z.L. Fiber that signified the supreme Butterfly paddle was in my hand. For real.

I did not even dream about having this kind of paddle. It belonged to the professional players, and they existed on another planet.

The teammates were just as mesmerized as they looked on silently.

Receiving such a fabulous gift was unquestionably a shred of success. I added it into my bottle of triumphs – something for disheartening days.

Dreamily, I nodded and thanked Coach.

He grinned, nodded, and stroked the back of my head. It sent a strong signal of safety in his presence. And it was the same sense of security Teacher Li gave me when he was next to me reading my composition back in Nan'an. It was the safety of being recognized.

As I turned to resume my previous spot, Wongji stood up.

His eyes and mine locked in an embrace.

My pulse raced, my palms perspired, and my cheeks flushed.

The paddle almost slipped out of my hand; I tightened my grip.

Our looks parted.

But there was a sharp sliver of something in Wongji's deep, dark eyes that I caught and would never let go of.

That something in his eyes permitted me to get on the bridge his earlier glimpses and visits had created for me.

And it encouraged me to walk on and cross a border – an invisible line in the middle of the bridge, in the fog – where I attained a limpid sense of awareness that I was lovable.

Coach took over the inner, Wongji's, room.

Starting from our first training session, Coach had me playing there. I should have been glad and grateful, but I was not. Instead, a weight began descending on my chest, making breathing hard. I did not want to get there solely because Coach liked me.

It had been my dream to earn my place in that inner room. In my mind's eye, I saw myself fighting through the foggy bridge with holes and hindrances and making it to the other side where Wongji awaited me.

Coach appointed Wongji as his assistant to lead two or three boys and practice on the outer table. From then on, Coach was always by my side. Starved for affection, I welcomed his excessive attention.

He stood close behind me and adjusted my playing gestures by holding my hands and repeating the moves. In this same manner, he taught me new techniques. I grew used to his sea breeze cologne and felt comfortable around him. As the sensory memory of my father was largely limited to his reek of tobacco and alcohol, it was great to receive Coach's refreshing scent and tender touches.

Coach often wore deep-blue jeans, and a white or pink or any light-colored polo shirt with its collar turned up. Such attire made him look younger, taller, and more handsome. There was an air of easy assurance and calm around him, as if he was totally in control. The sense of control and ease was the quality that I had yearned for in my father, probably since I was three.

Coach brought a large bag of balls and a serving machine that rapidly and continuously shot out balls. He would set the device with different intervals and program the balls to land at various spots. It was sometimes a long table (far from the net), sometimes a short table (close to the net), sometimes left, sometimes right, sometimes middle (the hardest, because your body was in your way as you tend to stand close to the center) and a mix-and-match of these shots. We had to stay incredibly focused and react fast.

I got to play the longest with the most variations.

Time went so swiftly: it had been three or four months that Coach's intensive training and protectiveness had been focused on me. He absorbed me completely.

One day, I looked around and realized Wongji was gone.

When my break came, I went to the office and asked the manager about it.

Keeping my voice low and steady, I tried to sound casual.

The manager told me that Wongji had left the team. The reason Wongji gave was that he needed to focus on his study. He said he would take the Hong Kong Certificate of Education Examination soon.

The news hit me like a violent slap to my face, making it flush.

Feeling the heat, I lowered my head, thanked the manager, and turned around.

I forced myself to put one foot before the other and keep walking.

Wongji had disappeared from my life for good. My bridge came tumbling down, and its debris fell on my chest, making it hard for me to breathe.

An uproar from my throat took on the form of a silent scream.

Tears of anguish and disappointment filled my eyes.

My head grew light, my feet heavy.

"Fongling!" Coach called.

I drew a few deep breaths, brushed off the tears, and recomposed myself. A moment or two afterward, I gathered myself up and walked back to the training room.

My body felt so heavy while my mind was getting gloomy.

And then, it was as if something had fallen out of my pocket.

I told myself it was just a tiny piece of tissue paper.

I kept moving forward and did not allow myself to look back.

Not even once.

After a year of rigorous training together, day in and day out, Coach became my avid adviser. Like a doting father, he seldom allowed me out of his sight for long during our training sessions.

Coach led our team, and we entered the East Kowloon table tennis competition.

When I won the third prize in the young women's single category, I wished Wongji were there. If so, we might have had a chance to win an award as a team.

I wanted my parents there and for them to be proud of me.

The manufacturing industry in Hong Kong was prosperous in the 1980s. My parents had a lot of work. They worked at the same Japanese electrical appliances production plant at first. Then, my mother moved on to garment and, later, food factories. My father stayed on and became a line supervisor. They both worked long hours, leaving home around 7am and returning around 9pm.

I would make sure to get home before 7pm. My parents neither asked me about my studies nor my life in general. They did not know anything about my table tennis playing or the existence of Coach.

In the second half of Primary Six, I needed to prepare for secondary school entry examinations. Only a few public secondary schools used English as the teaching medium and were highly regarded and desired. The competition was keen.

As a front runner in my school, I could get into a prominent English secondary school. It meant that, after graduation, entry into one of the two universities in Hong Kong would very much be within my reach.

However, Coach asked me to be brave and consider an alternative: the newly established professional athlete training college in Sha Tin. It provided a dormitory and would give me an independent life right away, ahead of my classmates or even my elder siblings.

More importantly, he kept telling me that if I joined such a school and received profound training in their state-of-the-art facilities, I would qualify for the official Hong Kong Junior Table Tennis Team.

Becoming a member of the official Hong Kong team overtook everything else. All I could think about was representing the region to play at overseas tournaments. What a glorious homecoming that would be! Such glory must be able to compensate for the years of humiliation and hardship that my parents had endured to raise us here. The prospect of making my parents proud and happy filled me with ineffable joy.

So I made up my mind and took Coach's suggestion to apply to the sports school.

Coach told me I would need to pass a medical checkup before applying.

I had never had a checkup before.

It sounded serious, frightening, like an operation.

Coach said he understood my fear. To help me, he said he could do a preliminary test for me by giving a quick check of my muscles and reflexes.

He told me that if he found nothing wrong with me, I would not need to bother my parents to take me to a clinic.

And even if he did find something wrong, he could help me solve it, he told me reassuringly. My parents would never need to know and be troubled.

He knew the thought of disturbing my parents concerned me the most and that I would take every opportunity to save them the trouble.

He had thought of everything. How nice of him. I was fourteen.

The Checkup

It was March 1989. One day, Coach called off the training early. He asked me to join him in his car and told me we would do the checkup at his home.

Coach often picked me up and drove me to competitions over the year. It was unusual to own a car in Hong Kong; only wealthy people could afford to do so. Hence, it was another extravagant treatment he had bestowed upon me, making me feel like a pearl in his palm.

Gladly, I got into his car that afternoon.

It took almost an hour to get to his home. As he was driving, he told me about his family – his two-year-old son and his wife, who was pregnant with their second child. He said his wife had taken their son to visit her mother that day.

When we arrived, I realized he lived far north of Kowloon, close to the Shenzhen border with mainland China.

I entered his apartment. He locked the door behind me.

A massive TV sat in the middle of the living room, looming.

"Fongling, do you like singing? I've got Karaoke equipment here."

Coach was removing his jacket when he asked this.

"Oh, it's okay. Maybe next time."

My voice sounded tremulous, thin, timorous – alien to my own ears.

The time now was our usual training hour.

We should still be in the center with the others.

Being alone with him for the first time in his home felt strange and uncomfortable.

It was as if I saw myself in a bizarre dream, but I could not reach out to wake her.

"Come, put your bag down here."

He pointed to a corner spot.

"We will be quick," he looked me in the eye and added.

Slowly, I let go of my bag.

"Fongling, come here. Stand straight and stretch out your arms, please."

I did as told.

He went and stood behind me.

His hands gave my shoulders a gentle squeeze.

"Good, keep your arms up for me for a few more moments."

His voice sounded calm and resolute. His breath was warm above my ears.

"I'm going to lower my hands now. Don't be scared. I need to inspect your chest."

His hands reached from behind in a slow-motion way and cupped my breasts.

I froze.

"Oh, sweetie, you are fourteen and not growing yet!"

He had never called me that and never made this kind of comment.

It was perplexing and disconcerting.

I stared straight in front, fearing to meet his eyes.

I was afraid I might find a stranger instead.

He kept his hands on my breasts.

I stood rigid like a scarecrow.

His fingers circled my breasts.

Sensing my discomfort, he said:

"Come with me, sweetie."

He moved toward the bedroom.

I dropped my arms and ran to the door.

He rushed back and grabbed my wrist.

We stayed motionless for a second or two.

He loosened his grip.

Tenderly, he pulled me into his arms and embraced me.

A moment later, he started to stroke my short hair.

Then he lowered his hand and put it on my naked neck.

The minute his iron-cold fingers touched the skin of my neck, I recoiled.

But he had one hand on my neck, another around the middle of my back.

He kept me tight and close to him.

The whiff of his cologne morphed into a wave of menace.

My body quivered.

Was it real or unreal?

"*Shh shh*, sweetie, calm down," he whispered while stroking my hair.

"I'm your Coach. Remember? You're the student I'm proudest of – my favorite."

Softly, he went on:

"I can't love you enough. Don't you know?"

He patted my back consolingly.

"I will never hurt you."

He continued to hold me tight to him.

He let go of my body and took my hand, leading me toward the bedroom.

I felt hypnotized and followed him meekly.

"Yes, sweetie, that's right. Come here and lie down. Make yourself comfortable."

I lay. Fear gripped and cramped my calves and stomach.

Something went through me – a pang so sharp my breath got stuck in my throat.

I swallowed hard and tried to breathe again.

He walked over to the other side of the bed.

Heavy brown cotton curtains hung next to a large window.

He drew them tightly together, shutting out the last dregs of the daylight.

His body approached me. His eyes came right above mine.

The tip of his nose brushed against mine as he said:

"Good girl."

He lowered himself and lay on his side next to me, propping himself up on his elbow.

He began caressing my brow with his hand.

Taking a tissue from the box on the bedside table, he carefully mopped away my sweat.

"Relax. The exam will be over before you know it," he said in a murmur.

A moment later, he sat up and went to the end of the bed.

"Sweetie, I'm going to take off your socks for you. You will feel more comfortable."

He did so tenderly.

"Okay, stay relaxed."

He continued:

"Now, I'm going to remove your panties."

My body wriggled.

"Relax. Be still. So I can examine you properly."

He lifted the hem of my white school dress.

I turned to my side, trying to sit up.

He hastened forward and pressed down my shoulders.

"Sweetie, don't worry. We're just going through a normal procedure."

He cooed and said:

"They will do the same thing to you in the clinic."

He stroked my forehead.

"Good girl, stay calm."

He climbed back onto the bed and knelt across my legs.

His hand reached for my panties and removed them in one quick pull.

My body curled up.

He leaned forward.

His upper body forced down on me, keeping me flat in bed.

His head was on my left shoulder.

Then, his right hand touched me – there – between my legs.

"No!" I screamed.

"*Shh, shh.*"

His hand stayed there and kept on touching.

"Please stop. I'm feeling sick!"

"Okay, if you calm down, we can take a break. Will you be calm?"

My head dropped. I was motionless.

He did not slacken his grip on me.

He moved a hand toward my abdomen and began massaging it.

"Good girl, keep cool. Let's try again and get this over with."

He knelt next to my waist, facing me.

Suddenly, he covered my mouth with one hand, and another attacked me there.

He increased his force. His breath became so hot it seared every inch of my skin.

I shook my head violently, trying to shake off his hand. It tightly sealed my mouth.

Then, he inserted his finger into me.

I shook my head again and again. My efforts were in vain.

His hand pressed down on my mouth harder and harder. He got more and more animated.

His eyes were fixated on that place.

Inch by inch, he drilled into me as if to break me open.

Forcefully, he thrust repeatedly inside me. Every motion of it was tearing me apart.

"Come on, sweetie. Relax. You will enjoy this!"

I wanted to vomit.

He was entirely focused on that part of mine. His hand that covered my mouth loosened.

I grasped the opportunity, sucked up as much air as possible, and shrieked:

"Stop!"

With every ounce of energy I still possessed, I fought to break free from him.

He used his whole upper body to hold me down.

"Be still, my girl. I want to take some secretion from you as a test sample."

I had no idea what he was talking about. What was "secretion"?

And right at that very moment, I noticed a scarier object lying on the bedside table.

A strip of glass.

It shone faintly and caught my eye.

As if he followed my eyes, he withdrew his finger and picked up that strip of glass.

"I'm going to put this in bed between your legs."

He added:

"I need to take your secretion, place it on this glass, and send it to the lab."

I gave up hope of breaking free now.

He might shove that strip of glass into me.

The thought paralyzed me.

He could gut me like a dead fish.

He reinserted his finger inside me and thrust hard.

My body was tight. Severe pains seized me.

A burning sensation rushed up. I felt like fainting.

But the intensity of the pain kept me awake.

Tears rolled down my cheeks and wet the pillow.

I looked up at the ceiling.

A cumbersome crystal chandelier seemed to manifest itself out of nowhere.

It looked so far above my body, existing on its own planet.

Its small decorative glass pieces felt like a cluster of stars throbbing against a dark sky.

My eyes drifted amid the branches of the stars, those small pieces of glass.

In their reflection, the man unbuckled, unzipped, and lowered his trousers.

He pulled up her dress, opened her legs, and put his tongue between them.

The muscles of her thighs became cramped. Her foot kicked.

He pressed her down and continued.

He moved up, climbing on top of her.

Her eyes were unable to close.

He twisted her head to one side.

She kept quiet.

He made all the noises.

The air was thick – salty, fishy smells seizing hold of the room.

His breathing got heavier; his hands grabbed at her breasts.

Then he gripped her neck.

He might strangle her.

His movements accelerated and accelerated further.

The buckle of his belt was striking her.

A cry joined the jingling of his buckle.

His body slumped down on her.

The sound of his heavy breaths persisted, dominating.

He dragged himself up.

When his body pulled away from hers, she felt something warm and slimy slide out.

It slipped down her inner thigh.

He held onto the top of his trousers, rushing out of the room.

Unquiet darkness seized the space, so heavy it could barely leave the ground.

When I heard my breathing again, I rolled up my body.

I put my feet on the floor and stood up. My legs wobbled. Piercing pain from that place between my legs came in waves. I fell back on the bed, waiting for the pain to pass.

Realizing I did not have my panties, I looked around. They were white, partly torn in an inner corner of the bed. Reaching out to retrieve them, I noticed the bloodstains on the bedsheet and wondered when I bled.

My head felt light. Eager to get out of the room, I focused on putting my panties back on.

And then, I smoothed out my dress and gathered all my energy, forcing myself to keep walking and facing the front.

My body doubled up near the door. I clutched my abdomen with one hand and the other supported my back. Step by step, agonizingly, I shifted my body toward the toilet. It was right next to the bedroom.

The burning sensation assailed me yet again. It made me retch. My sweat-drenched body shuddered, and my legs shook so hard I could not move forward. Standing with my eyes closed for a moment or two, I took a few deep breaths, gritted my teeth, and walked out of the room. Eventually, I made it to the bathroom.

Slumping down on the toilet seat, I felt the redundancy of my body. I wished it would dissolve and drop into the pot. Then, I could just flush it away.

Half floating, I managed to stagger out to the living room and sat on the floor next to my bag. I picked it up and gripped it – the remains of my dignity.

He was leaning on the rail of the balcony, smoking.

It was my first time seeing him smoke. But I was not surprised.

It felt like nothing he did would surprise me anymore.

My eyes tottered. I tried to steady them by fixing them on his back.

Then I began wondering who he was and what had happened.

It was a nightmare – a night terror, and that must be it. That was all.

I repeated this line of thought to myself, trying to convince myself.

It was just a night of terror. I would get over it. For sure, I would.

Everything would return to normal again.

My eyes continued to transfix on his back.

All the surroundings, including myself, including him, felt like illusions.

Incomprehensible.

Yet, the excruciating pain at that place was sharp and urgent.

It was as if something kept drilling, tearing me apart.

The familiarly strange figure in front of me dragged on his cigarette.

He inhaled the chemicals like they were his life support.

The smoke that he exhaled swirled upwards and hung in the air.

Then it shifted like ghosts in the breeze, curling into nothingness, gone without a trace.

His back moved as if he suddenly realized that I was sitting somewhere behind him. And that I was staring at him. He drew another drag of the cigarette and quenched it.

His body lowered. He reached his hand behind a big potted plant and hid his tiny ashtray.

Standing back up, he turned around, walked into the living room, and picked up his keys.

He avoided my eyes the whole time.

When he reached the door, he said:

"Let's go."

Part Two: Origin

Fujian, China

1974 – 1986

Wouling

The breeze of dawn woke Chan Wingwai, my mother. The air was crisp and cool. A riot of red, white, and yellow chrysanthemums blossomed outside the window, releasing profound perfume.

Wingwai was eight-and-a-half-months pregnant. She opened her eyes, inhaled the aromatic air, exhaled slowly, and smiled. But a pang shot through her abdomen. She took a few deep breaths. The pang ceased. She thought about going to the toilet, so she shifted and struggled to sit up. The alarm clock on her bedside table indicated seven-something when she glimpsed it.

Wingwai's mother, my Grandma Chan, had come from Nan'an to Datian county, to help her. Grandma Chan was in the living room when she heard sounds of discomfort coming from her daughter's bedroom. She hastened there.

Once Grandma's slim figure appeared in the doorway, Wingwai sighed with relief. As Grandma approached, Wingwai saw the concerned look on her mother's face. She beamed a little and said, "*Ma, moyaogin*," in Hokkien dialect to reassure her mother that she was okay.

Grandma leaned forward and mopped the sweat from Wingwai's brow with her handkerchief. She then gently touched her daughter's belly. Wingwai grinned and told her mother it was just a minor stomach ache she was having.

Grandma thought it might be more than that. "*Danlet*," she whispered to her daughter, "Hold on," and told her that it was better to have the nurse come and do a quick checkup.

Grandma helped Wingwai lie back down, tucked her in, cleared the hair away from her forehead, and ensured her daughter was comfortable.

Grandma stole another concerned look at her daughter before she hurried off to fetch the nurse.

Nurse Xia also acted as a midwife. Her room was only a few minutes away. She rushed in with Grandma. After inspecting Wingwai, Nurse Xia yelled:

"Yaoshengler, yaoshengler!"

She cried out in Mandarin, announcing the baby's arrival.

Grandma froze. She suddenly forgot how to react. Nurse Xia calmed herself and took charge of the situation. She asked Grandma to bring towels, boil water, and arrange other things to deliver the baby.

Wah! A loud cry broke out at around 9am. I declared my arrival in this world.

It was 20 October 1974, the year of the tiger.

My family name is Leung, which means wooden beams, and my first name is Fongling.

Fong means fragrance; *Ling* exquisite.

Based on my mother's narration, I reconstructed my birth scene as above. She often ended the story by saying I came rushing into this world and did not bring her too much pain. I will treasure these words until I die because they represent the rarest thing my mother has for me: approval.

Mother said I was born with a head of wild, thick hair, a pair of bright, piercing eyes, and a dark complexion, unlike the rest of the family. They nicknamed me *Wouling*, "Dark Ling" in Hokkien. Chinese dislike dark skin. They think it resembles that of laborers who work under the sun. They envy rich people or famous scholars who enjoy pleasant indoor lives. They praise these rich and famous people for having silken white skin. I was born second-rate.

Leung Wailai

Leung Wailai, my late father, was absent from my birth, just like he would be absent most of my life. We never had one intimate father-daughter talk. And yet, his influence loomed immensely in my life and continues after his death.

In a few of his remaining old photographs, Father looked like a Chinese version of the young Goethe. They both had a high forehead, a pair of bright, piercing eyes, a tall, straight nose, and relatively thin but expressive lips. Father also had a head of wild, wavy hair inherited from his Indonesian-born father, Grandpa Leung.

Father's tousled hair and distinctive facial features gave impressions of rebellion and wildness. Also, the villagers from his hometown, Nan'an, often mistook him for a mixed-race person. But he was a very restrained person who highly respected traditional Chinese values. For instance, being the eldest of six siblings, he endeavored to act appropriately and conduct himself as a model of virtue. However, his sultry looks seemed to tell another story – one that allowed him to live in an exotic dream in a foreign land of his own. Grandpa and Grandma Leung also left him alone and treated him like an adult early on due to his eldest son status.

Father was born in 1947 in China. He enjoyed the privileged life of a *qiaomin*, an overseas returned Chinese family. Foreigners were scarce in mainland China, especially in the old days and in small southern villages like my father's. Foreigners represented wealthy and advanced lives; therefore, the villagers regarded them highly. So, those Chinese who slightly resembled foreigners or overseas returned Chinese tended to enjoy a more privileged life. It was because of my great-grandpa, who had made a fortune in Indonesia and contributed to the development of the new China.

Father's hometown was full of pragmatic villagers who worshiped wealth. But such a privileged life did not sit well with my father.

Through his boyhood and early adulthood, Father appeared torn between the free spirit inherited from his foreign-born father and the restricted teachings of his motherland.

Confucianism remained influential in rural areas down south, far away from Beijing, the capital up north. The countryside people regarded Confucius as their respected ancestor and saw Communism as their new adoptive parents who controlled their daily lives.

To the villagers, the Party was not different from the emperors of the past. They were used to obeying the emperors and felt compelled to follow the Party.

As long as the Party united China and they could have *Yi Kou Fan Chi* [a mouthful of rice to eat, i.e. the means to live] they abided by the new ruler's rules. But deep down, they continued to rely on the wisdom of their ancient ancestor.

When my father was young, he behaved happily and freely one minute and turned into a moody, withdrawn person the next. As a second-year junior high school student, he suffered from a mental breakdown, stayed home for two years, and avoided social contact with outsiders. But he did not rest. Instead, he became an avid reader and devoured all the world-renowned novels.

He read the Chinese versions of those novels and often commented fervently about those stories in his diaries. The pages inside those diaries looked scratchy with his illegible handwriting, which conveyed the feeling of a caged wild animal trying to escape.

Chinese writing paper usually has squares printed on it for one to write each character within the boundaries. The handwriting of my father often fled out of those squares.

Father's favorite novel was *Doctor Zhivago*. Yuri Zhivago's sense of loneliness and insecurity and the book's lamentation of reality's unpredictability appealed greatly to my father. Inspired by Yuri, Father also wanted to become a doctor. And because of his brightness, he got into medical school – one of a few in Fujian province – and became a doctor.

Father wrote poems also. But he did not aspire to be a poet like Yuri. Also, unlike Yuri, Father was never eager to seek companions, even female ones. He was content with his own company. Often, he appeared to immerse himself in a big book, alone, in the corner of a park, on the soft ground with fallen leaves wafting around him from time to time, one or two laying atop his shoulders serenely.

Influenced by the books he read and being the eldest son of a prominent family, my father often felt that he carried massive responsibility. He perceived himself as the role model for his brothers, sister, and the county's people who looked up to his family. Therefore, he held a high view of propriety and morality and paid additional attention to *Lai* – custom, manners, and courtesy – an integral part of his reputation.

When he became a doctor in 1969, he became a government employee, because the Party administered all employment in China.

The Party allocated my father to a remote mountainous area, and he worked as a residential doctor in a prefectural hospital. Another doctor worked with him, and the head of the hospital supervised them.

My parents, my two elder siblings, me, and later, a younger one, lived in the hospital's staff quarters. It was in those staff quarters that I was born.

As my father's third child and second daughter, I attribute these qualities of mine – the love of literature, the passion for reading, the wildness in my blood, the inability to fit in, the tendency to dramatic mood swings, the overwhelming sense of responsibility – to my father, the one and only Leung Wailai.

Chan Wingwai

"Knotty" comes to my mind when I recall my relationship with my mother.

Unlike my father, she was very present throughout my childhood. And yet, such presence was poisonous to me as it often made me hate myself because I got on her nerves and never seemed lovable to her and, by extension, to others.

My mother, Chan Wingwai, passionate and patriotic, was born in 1948. She took great pride in it and often told people that she shared the same age as the new People's Republic of China. And so, she earned the nickname Red Girl for her fiery temper and patriotic spirit.

When she attended primary school, she became a member of the Young Pioneers. And later, when she studied in a teacher's training institution, she became a Red Guard during the Cultural Revolution.

Like many zealous Red Guards, she traveled as a school representative with a highly-regarded delegation to Mao's hometown, Shaoshan, in Hunan province. She then managed to arrive at Tiananmen Square and saw Chairman Mao.

In November 1966, the moment Mao appeared on the balcony of the square, she was one among myriads of the Red Guards who roared:

"Long live Chairman Mao!"

Like tens of thousands of the Red Guards in the square, she fanatically waved the Little Red Book – the quotations of Mao – and completely immersed herself in this period of Mao's rule.

My mother's favorite writer was Lu Xun. In particular, she admired Lu's *Call to Arms*. It is a collection of short stories with two most popular ones – *Diary of a Madman* and *The True Story of Ah Q*.

The Party also valued Lu's traits, including the fact that he radically rejected China's past association with the Confucian system of ethics underpinning the old empires. Instead, he embraced something new and radical. So they glorified him by strengthening his teaching and promoting his progressive image through propaganda. They used the writer's immense influence over the young radicals to solidify their authority.

As a fervent follower of the Party, my mother took everything it imposed as the highest wisdom, purest truth. So, she looked up to Lu Xun and read and reread his *Call to Arms* to keep herself aligned with the Party.

From 1969, a relatively calmer political climate ensued, even as the Cultural Revolution continued. That year, my mother began her career as a primary school teacher, and my father started working as a doctor.

My mother's dream came true when she took on the teacher role. Educating the country's new generation was the wondrous way that she thought she could serve the glorious Party. Like the Party, she wished to transform people's lives, especially the poor ones.

With such a dedicated, nationalistic mother, I became an ardent admirer of the People's Republic of China myself.

When I lived in British-administered Hong Kong in my early teens, I had a potent reaction upon hearing the Chinese national anthem.

Whenever the horn's piercing sound reached my ears, I rose and stood straight. And I sang along to the exhilarating lyrics – "*Qilai! Buyuan zuo nuli de renmen*" – that followed.

"Arise, you who refuse to be slaves."

Singing the anthem, *Yiyongjun Jinxingqu*, or *March of the Volunteers*, I felt every body cell vibrating with the song's vigorous rhythm.

Adrenaline ran through my veins and brought tears to my eyes.

I continued, "With our flesh and blood, let us build a new Great Wall!"

My back straight, my head high; my hands trembled with profound pride in the Motherland while tears rolled down my cheeks. Like my mother, I was prone to tears.

And I had her face, her voice, her petite hands.

But I never had her unconditional love.

My mother seemed to dislike me because I was darker, and my character resembled my father's the most, and since my mother never loved my father, I, too, became unlovable.

My mother could not stand me. She and my father had an arranged marriage. And, for my mother, it was a marriage without love.

Despite everything, I love my mother.

Amid the Guava Groves

We lived in the dormitory where I was born, at the hospital where my father worked, until I was three. Then we moved over to the dormitory at the school where my mother taught.

We lived in the Jiyang *Xiang*, (officially a township, but really just a village) in Datian county. It took us about twelve hours by bus and then another ten hours on foot to reach there from my parents' hometown in Nan'an because only mountain trails were available for that second half of the journey.

The village was poverty-stricken; villagers struggled to have one meal a day. But my family had a good quality of life because the villagers respected us. They considered my parents – a doctor and a teacher – the esteemed *Zhi Shi Fen Zi* [educated people]. They appreciated the wonderfully compassionate Party who appointed these elites to the poor villages to liberate them. So we enjoyed a high social status.

My earliest memory of living in Jiyang is from when I was three or four.

A villager who lived near the school and made tofu offered my family some of it, freshly-made and warm, in the morning from time to time. The homemade tofu was full of the rich fragrance of the yellow beans. When the newly-made tofu arrived at around dawn, delicate and warm, in an enamel bowl, I would sneak out of bed, stand on tiptoe, wrap my hands around it, and launch my nose at the tofu to breathe in its awesome aroma. Once the sublime scent filled my nostrils, I was a lamb frolicking in the field all day.

Another advantage of spending my early childhood in my mother's school dormitory was that the classrooms became my playground. As the treasured Teacher Chan's daughter, I often ran in and out of the classrooms while the classes took place.

The teachers never complained. The students fought to attract my attention. They felt triumphant if I chose to sit among them. Then they would give me whatever they had, like small smooth rocks in interesting shapes, to play with so I would sit with them longer.

A tall, young male teacher often played run and catch with me during recess in the schoolyard. I ran my heart out, giggling. After a few rounds, he captured and held me for some time. Then he would pick me up, rub his rough, fibrous chin against my cheeks, and tickle me to death. I wriggled, and we both laughed so hard that our laughter filled the schoolyard.

The students were impoverished. They dressed in rags, and even with their emaciated bodies, the tops barely covered their belly buttons on the bone-chilling and often wet winter days, a pair of silvery snotty trails hanging below their noses.

These poor students usually came to school barefoot. They carried a small warm pot – a bamboo-made, oval-shaped basket with a small metal bowl in the middle. Inside the bowl, there were a few small pieces of burning coal. They put the pot in between their thighs during class.

Some students got watery congee for breakfast, while many could not even afford that. Their eyes focused on the blackboard with tired looks.

Most of these deprived students still strove to listen to the class and copied words from the blackboard. Their hands trembled so hard that their palms could scarcely hold the tiny pencil.

After finishing writing, they quickly put down the pencils and returned their freezing hands to the pot for whatever infinitesimal warmth they could get.

Guava tree groves grew around the school's playground. Undersized dark green fruits hung on the thin branches.

The experience of eating unripe guava was not pleasant. The immature guava was so hard that your teeth felt weak, biting in, and it was so tart that your palate itched. It tasted like tree bark with a small amount of explosive sour juice that rushed toward the back of your throat. The aftertaste was a scratchy sensation that disturbed every sense of your body.

We, the children, had no snacks. So whenever we were hungry after school, we would try to eat one of the never-ripe guavas and regret it soon afterward. But at least at the moment of need, the hard, small guavas were there and ready to help us combat hunger.

Unlike my poor little playmates, who had no guarantee of food at home, I could always return to the school's dormitory and would have dinner awaiting me.

Teacher Chan and Doctor Leung both had "iron rice bowls," having secure government jobs, and as their daughter, the Party also provided me with the essential means of living.

I was entitled to the following tickets or rations. Each month, for rice, I got seven catties to start (1 catty in modern mainland China is 500 grams). When I turned twelve, the quantity increased to eleven catties; it would then rise yearly by a further two catties, then stay at twenty-two for a few years before reaching its summit and plateauing out at twenty-eight catties, the standard quantity for a full-grown adult. For oil, I got three *liang* (1 *liang* or *tael* is 50 grams) each month. For cloth, every year, I could have fourteen feet.

These entitlements further enhanced my pride in being my parents' child. The guava tree of pride and sorrow was my constant childhood companion.

The Moon Festival

I have loved the Moon Festival since I was a child.

It has a less poetic name, the Mid-Autumn Festival, and it happens when the moon is at its roundest and brightest in the year, around September in the western calendar.

The festival was to express gratitude for a plenteous harvest in the past. Now it is just another occasion for gathering. It makes me nostalgic for the Moon Festival during my childhood days.

When I was five or six, the teachers and my family gathered together on the Moon Festival day's early evening. We brought out the tables and chairs from the classroom and lined them up in the middle of the schoolyard, preparing to enjoy the best view of the moon.

My mother brought out two pots brimming with hot *Tie Guan Yin*, "Iron Buddha" tea, her hometown specialty. The headmaster contributed the *yuebing*, "moon cakes," and other teachers shared various round-shaped fruits mirroring the moon.

A tray bearing two dozen moon cakes and another tray of fruits, teapots, teacups, and plates crowded the table. The headmaster put a fist-size porcelain rabbit as the centerpiece to complete the setting.

"Ah, the Jade Rabbit."

A teacher who was a lover of myths uttered the words movingly.

She raised her head to the moon, beholding it. It was as if she was witnessing the transformation of the rabbit right there and then.

We took our places at the table and admired the luminous orb in the deep blue sky. Even we kids quietened down under the mesmerizing moonlight and behaved like mini-adults.

The myth-loving teacher sat amid my friends and me and told us that our ancestors had a particular belief about the full moon. They believed the image of a short-tailed rabbit playing under an osmanthus shrub presented itself on the surface of the super big, bright, round moon.

The teacher had a soft, mellifluous voice which, combined with her dreamy eyes, drew us into her world. Our attentive eyes held the sheen of the moon as she began recounting this fabulous tale.

One day, Buddha assumed the form of a bodhisattva and appeared in a forest glade, where he made a fire to warm himself. The bodhisattva told the animals living there that he was hungry and thirsty and asked them for food and drink.

The otter brought him seven pieces of fish. The jackal shared part of his kill. When it was the rabbit's turn, the timid creature deeply regretted that he could give only herbs and grasses, the simple food he ate. Noticing the fire, the rabbit realized that there was something more he could offer. With that thought, he jumped into the flames.

For this selfless act, the Buddha announced that the image of the rabbit would forever emblazon the moon's surface as a shining example of modesty, compassion, and self-sacrifice.

The young me neither understood those three big words at the end nor the moral of the story. But the illuminating moon, so pristine and complete, sparked hope in me.

Turning around, I saw my father and mother sitting peacefully together and sipping at their tea. Silently, I pleaded:

"Dear Jade Rabbit, please help me ask the magnificent moon to shine her light on me. That way, I can become a bright, white, and pretty girl. My parents will be proud of me. Please, Jade Rabbit. Please!"

I looked up to the moon, searching for the rabbit and drinking in the brightness of the moonlight. Then, I closed my eyes to try and retain such illumination within me.

If only I could shine, I would be worthy of my parents' love.

Cupping my face, I listened to the adults chatting and children giggling.

The playground was shrouded in perfection.

Half-awake and half-dreaming, I blanketed myself with the moonlight.

A sense of felicity filled the chambers of my heart.

Beneath the full moon, everything was pure and possible.

A Little Lightbulb

Growing up, I adored and feared my parents. Just as they disliked me, I detested myself.

My mother, Teacher Chan, was a prominent teacher in our county and beyond.

"Fongling, your mother is my favorite teacher! I only pay attention to her class," Luk, the naughtiest student of my mother, told me.

"Your mother's class is never boring. She teaches us how to write Chinese characters in her unique, fascinating ways that help me learn and remember them better," another student, Jianing, agreed and said, "Luk is right. Like the word 随 [which means "follow" and is composed from: 阝 ears; 辶 a boat or to go; 有 have], Teacher Chan creates a chant that goes: do you have ears? If you do, please come with me. I will never forget how to write that difficult word again."

Mother was one of just three official teachers in the whole school.

A few locally appointed secondary-school graduates – "barefoot teachers" – helped take up some minor classes, but they were not government employees like my mother. The local government recruited these less qualified candidates, offering them temporary teaching positions in response to the party's newly implemented provisional policy due to the severe shortage of teachers after the Cultural Revolution.

My mother taught Chinese and Music from primary one to three with two classes consisting of forty to fifty students each. Many children dropped out after the third grade (around age eight) because they became farmhands, their families putting them to work in the paddy fields. And my mother was the class teacher for all these big classes. She taught from early morning to late afternoon and attended to the slower-learning students after school. She then corrected the students' homework at night after going to bed.

At the same time, my mother never missed her housework. Despite heavy workloads and endless family duties, she remained a devoted teacher and an admirable woman in the public eye. Unfortunately, her treatment of the object of her scorn, me, was different. For instance, she often got very annoyed with me and scolded me:

"Why do you have to stare at me with your big hateful eyes whenever I correct you with something? Why can't you smile and nod as your brother does? Once I see his smile and nod, my anger evaporates. But you look at me with your big eyes full of accusation like I'm doing you a great injustice. It disgusts me and makes me dislike you more!"

My eyes were average. It made me wonder if Mother ever really saw me.

My head dropped, and my shoulders sank at her words.

I forced back my tears.

There was no way I could ever behave like Brother. No, even if I could act like my brother, I would never be able to please my mother as he did. She knew that; we both knew that. He was her favorite. She lavished most of her love on him and treated him like the man in her life. It was partly due to gender preference but more so because of her discontent with my father. It was her way of telling him that he could never be as close to her as their son.

To avoid our family's chaos, my elder sister left for boarding school once her secondary school started. Being the youngest and loveliest, my younger sister was the pearl in my mother's palm. She could get away with anything, while I always got into trouble.

For instance, if we both got our clothes dirty after wearing them for a day, our mother would only scold me for giving her extra work. I knew she expected us to wear the clothes for two days in winter as she hardly had time and energy to hand-wash the whole family's laundry.

I did feel sorry and tried to help her. But she just brushed me aside like brushing off an annoying fly. I must have been around six.

*

As for my father, at work he was a well-respected doctor to his patients, his colleagues, and the hospital's head, and at home a distant, austere man.

If I did not address Father once in a whole year, he probably would not have noticed.

I was afraid of him and would try my best to stay out of his way. Once, I caught his attention by not holding my chopsticks properly.

Enraged, he gritted his teeth and gave me a repulsed look. In a low, deep, penetrative tone and a slow, deliberate, unreserved way, he said:

"You are such bad mud that you cannot stick on the wall!"

His words stuck in my head.

The incident was reminiscent of a scene from *Dream of the Red Chamber*. The core character of *Dream* is Baoyu, who fears his father, Zheng Jia.

Zheng Jia is an aristocrat and a Confucian scholar. He despises Baoyu as he finds him useless. He thinks Baoyu does nothing all day except fool around with girls, his cousins, and young maids.

My father's words reminded me of the scene when Baoyu starts attending a private school. It happens on that first school day morning when he goes to greet his father.

Baoyu and his father have different dwellings. When he arrives at his father's residence and stands outside his father's living room, his legs violently shake. He has to steady himself by holding onto a door frame.

His father is talking with some high-ranking officials and reputable scholars. When he glimpses the sight of his son, he barks:

"What are you doing here?"

Baoyu manages to control his fear and answers in a trembling voice:

"Father, I come to bid you good morning. Today is my first day of attending school."

"You attend school? If I hear you mention that again, I will die of shame."

He carries on, "Go and do your usual thing – play. Your standing there is staining my carpet; your holding of my door frame is soiling it! You, useless thing, get out of my sight!"

As *Dream of the Red Chamber* is autobiographical, I felt for the writer. It was a relief to learn that I was not alone. Cao Xuequi, or Baoyu, was wounded by his father, who never once tried to understand and love him for who he was.

My father could be another Zheng Jia who took his unconventional son for granted and would not realize his value until too late.

Baoyu disappears after achieving what his father wanted him to succeed and reappears in the book's final scene, giving three kowtows to his father before he departs with a priest to become a monk and leaves home for good. When Baoyu is gone without a trace, Zheng Jia realizes Baoyu was much nobler than he could ever have been and grander than he could ever have imagined.

Father loved Mother and remained lovelorn throughout his life with her.

He fell in love with her during their first official meeting in her house, which my maternal grandmother, Grandma Chan, arranged. Being respectful and loving her mother deeply, Mother accepted the arrangement readily.

During the first encounter, Mother was lively and lovely. She immediately became a muse to my father and inspired him to write poems like *Little Sparrow, Ode to Spring, Abide by You* to her.

Father also sent Mother numerous love letters to tell her that she was the love of his life, that she was the sparrow that awoke him from his state of hibernation, and that if she did not marry him, he would commit suicide.

Rather than being touched by his passionate admiration, she found him needy and his love declarations perturbing. She heard from their mutual friends that he was an extremist capable of carrying out his suicide threat. But then she trusted her mother – whoever her mother chose for her must be meritorious.

Also, Mother believed in fate. When she was a schoolgirl, she visited my father's home – the famous Leung's Mansion – on a school trip. Upon entering the mansion for the first time, she felt the strangest sense of familiarity, like she had visited there in her last life or dreams.

After a short day's visit, as she exited the house, she thought she would be back and not just as a visitor. She belonged there.

So, she told herself repeatedly that she could work on her feelings and that once they got married, time would be on her side and give her opportunities to develop more profound and favorable feelings toward him.

The shaky ground that their marriage started on got even worse for Mother.

She learned how manipulative Father was. As the eldest son of an illustrious family, Father was used to getting things his way.

When Father did not feel Mother loved him as he deserved, his mental state became unstable. Father often rummaged through Mother's letters, suspecting her of corresponding with someone else.

Father imagined and convinced himself that Mother did not return his love because she had another lover. His depression and anxiety worsened, and his drinking increased. He became a demanding husband and an angry, inaccessible father.

As I grew, I looked more and more like Mother, which troubled Father. And my characteristics – my large and wild handwriting, my love of eating raw garlic and coriander – resembled Father, which upset Mother. To both of them, everything I did seemed wrong. I seemed wrong.

Being a neurotic kid, I was frightened of the dark and often cried myself to sleep at night. But I did it softly, quietly, to avoid anyone noticing it. One day, Father installed a lightbulb on the wall above my bed. It was the most significant thing he had ever done for me.

Yet, the distance between us remained.

We grew further apart as time went by. Father retreated to his study while I tried to avoid attracting his attention.

When I missed Father, I would stare at the lightbulb during the night and reassure myself that he did care about me. But the muddy yellowish halo kept its distance.

The little lightbulb gazed back at me feebly, reluctantly.

Deep into the night, I often raised a hand and reached out to the gentle corona.

The lightbulb disappeared behind my palm.

A White Daisy Dress

My father needed to perform home visits to bedridden or old and frail patients. Sometimes, he went to distant and remote villages and could not make it back in a day.

During his absent nights, my mother appeared to be lighter and happier. Our little dormitory adopted a festive mood. We would have dinner early, wash up, and gather around her bed. It was a delicious story time.

Mother would tell us Grandma Chan's story, stories of her own younger self, or novels she read. Elder Brother and Younger Sister would always occupy the seats on either side of Mother. Elder Sister sat next to Younger Sister. They told me there was no space for me and asked me to go and sit on the other side.

The other side, away from them, was where they assigned me.

Nevertheless, I treasured the opportunity of having physical contact with Mother, even if it was only her feet that I could touch.

I sat low, hugging Mother's legs. On one of those nights, she told us about an English murder mystery at a mysterious old castle. When the antique clock inside the castle chimed midnight, the killer would start mounting the steps, putting his heavy feet one after another, toward the second-floor room where the protagonist was supposed to be asleep.

It was one of her favorites, and no matter how many times she retold it, she always managed to scare herself and us equally.

Somehow, after she started the story this time, I dozed off. Then I felt a kick and woke, realizing I had bitten into Mother's big toe. Her kick pained my lower jaw, and my siblings' laughter roused me further. I sensed the shame scorching my face.

*

I was seven. Unusually, one day, I accompanied Mother to the post office.

It was on the village's main street and among some *gong-xiao-she* [government-run supply and marketing cooperatives] in the form of small retail shops. The shops included a clothes outlet, a grocery store, a barbershop, and a farm tools store.

The day was bright, and yet the shops looked dusty and drowsy.

When Mother and I passed by the clothes shop, I peered in.

The clothes were all in cheerless colors and boring designs or no design. They were in the uniform style of plain white shirts and gray, dark blue, or black trousers for men and women alike that was expected at that time.

A voice in my head murmured: If I could not avoid wearing these clothes when I grew up, I would rather be a kid all my life.

But then, a child's white dress hanging above the counter, close to the ceiling, caught my attention. It was so precious and princess-like that it immediately cast a magic spell on me.

The dress had a pair of lovely round collars and a wavy hem with daisy embroidery. The petals were touching each other as if they were holding hands. The daisies looked happy and energetic with their wide-open white petals and yellow hearts.

The daisies made the dress come alive.

I pulled on the edge of Mother's blouse and exclaimed:

"Mother, look, what a beautiful dress!"

Annoyed, she gave it a quick look and replied:

"Yeah, okay, let's go."

"Mother… would you buy it for me, please?"

"Buy it for you? Don't be kidding. We don't have any extra money. And even if we have, the dress is not suitable for you. It's only fit for your younger sister."

She turned and walked on, ignoring me.

Like a balloon suddenly bursting and flying wildly a bit further before smashing its remains hard onto the ground – I was giddy with a heavy sense of defeat.

Bam! The balloon burst. *Pit!* Its remains hit the ground.

Bam! Pit! These were the noises of Mother's loud and clear rejection.

My ears were buzzing.

I tried in vain to shake off the blast in my head.

Gradually, I dragged myself behind her.

My mind refused to let go of the dress.

No, I would never let it go.

My eyes kept turning back and fixing on the dress.

Through backward glances, I attempted to implant the image of the exquisite dress into my brain. This way, I could own it and wear it in my dreams.

And in those dreams, I might be able to live a different life – one where I could feel that I was as exquisite as my younger sister and other siblings and as worthy of love as they were to my mother and father.

Bam! Pit! The sound often rang inside my head, waking me from those delicious dreams.

Under the Lychee Trees

M y parents applied to immigrate to Hong Kong before I was born. The approval came when I was ten and my younger sister eight. My parents took the two elder siblings and moved to Hong Kong first. They did that because the permit did not include my younger sister and me, as we had not yet been born and were not part of the application. Also, they did not try to add us immediately and appeal because they could not afford to take all four of us at once.

While my parents and two elder siblings left for Hong Kong, my younger sister and I had to continue our lives in the unfamiliar Nan'an county, my parents' home town.

We stayed behind for two and a half years.

Grandma Leung, whom I had met only five times previously when my parents brought us back to visit her and other relatives during Chinese New Year, became our guardian.

My parents and elder siblings departed on 29 December 1984.

A farewell crowd gathered around my younger sister and me on that icy-cold early morning. We assembled underneath the two lychee trees in front of Leung's Mansion, named after my wealthy great-grandfather who had ordered its construction.

The lushness of the evergreen lychee tree foliage, the heavy black clouds, the shiny white pickup car, and the grayness of the rice paddy fields full of dead stalks – the bleakness of it all – closed in on me, suffocating me.

Furthermore, the stomach-turning odor of the pig farms next to our house and the quiet, gripping sobs of the farewell throng added a tremendous weight to my already overburdened chest.

A tall, broad-shouldered aunt bent forward and grasped me around my waist. I fought to wriggle free from her. She then gripped me and used the other hand to pull my head toward her long winter coat. The stiff fiber of her overcoat hurt my face. But she kept pressing my head to her to prevent me from seeing my parents, elder sister, and brother leave.

Out of the corner of my eye, I saw Younger Sister fighting hard. She panicked, appearing not to comprehend what was happening.

As the pearl in my mother's palm, Younger Sister could not understand why she had to stay behind, like me, instead of going with them. Unlike me, she got to attend all the family excursions.

"I want Mama, I want Mama!" she shrieked.

She is two years younger than me. From that time on, she could only rely on me. I should have stopped crying. I should have comforted her. I should have fought off the fears for both of us. But I could not. Tears kept rolling from my eyes. With anger and despair, I felt my restrained body tremble. Frustration consumed me as I could not reach out to her, could not reduce her pain, and stop both of us from crying our hearts out.

My aunt's grip was forceful enough that it felt like she could snap my arms in half. But this fear did not stop me from keeping up my struggle.

Younger Sister and I broke free and chased the car. A few aunts and uncles ran after us. Once they seized us, they held us tight. We wailed. We begged. We kicked. Nothing worked. The car got smaller and disappeared behind a steep slope.

I thought I would never see them again.

I did not understand then why I was left behind. I thought I must have done something wrong. My parents and elder siblings had abandoned me. I was unwanted.

The sense of abandonment expanded in the context of Leung's Mansion, a monster to me. I moved in there on a dark, cold, late winter's day.

Entering the mansion from the side gate underneath the lychee trees, I first encountered a gloomy, narrow corridor. The darkness engulfed me, scaring me to tears.

Inside that dark passage, I did not know what I stepped on and what my hands touched. And worst of all, I could not see anything in front.

Somehow, I made it through and reached the left wing of the house.

This left side consisted of two sections: one portion was on a lower ground area with a well and three kitchens next to it; the other segment occupied a higher ground location, and it was a two-story compound with three rooms on each of the two floors.

After the left wing, I arrived at the main house. A right wing was next to the main house, and it comprised nine more rooms that served as guestrooms, kitchens, and storerooms.

The main house contained twelve large rooms, an upper grand hall, a central or inner courtyard, and a lower hall.

A majestic main gate stood at the end of the lower lobby. It opened onto a rectangular, giant, gray threshing ground that separated the mansion from others.

Next to the threshing area stood the two lychee trees.

Each summer, the trees produced bunches of sweet fruit that hung like over-sized, rose-colored grapes bathing in the sunshine.

Lychees, which have a short season, are generally believed to bring out the "fire" in people. As a Chinese saying goes, one lychee contains three batches of fire.

A Daoist altar solemnly sat inside the house at the back of the upper grand hall. Next to the altar, two photos of my great-grandparents appeared high up on the wall.

One day, I stood, threw back my head, and checked out the pictures.

My great-grandmother, the archetype of a Chinese "big wife" or the first wife of a prosperous household head, looked prim, proper, and unremarkable – an ethereal good wife.

My great-grandfather, Leung Shiurui, a successful businessman and philanthropist in Indonesia, had a grand and imposing look that matched his reputation. His face was slim, his cheekbones high.

The minute my eyes met my great-grandfather's, I froze. Our eyes overlapped.

I realized where my father got his looks and where I got mine.

A sense of security rose from within: I belonged to a large and reputable family.

The thought pleased me. It allowed me to bask in the illusion that I was meant to return to this mansion to claim and enjoy my high social status as a precious Ms. Leung.

Only when I was a grown woman did I learn that the daughters' names would not enter the book of Leung's family genealogy.

The earlier sense of security and belonging turned out to be a mirage.

It was the mirage in the desert of my wanting to feel that I was somebody – somebody who was deeply rooted.

My father had a younger sister and five younger brothers. My aunt had married and left Leung's Mansion long before.

When my younger sister and I arrived, three of the five uncles were married and lived in the house with Grandma Leung. Her husband, my Grandpa Leung, had left for Hong Kong two years before my parents did.

Grandma, Younger Sister, and I shared the same fate: the abandoned ones.

Grandma came from Yunnan province, southwestern China, miles away from Fujian. The dialects of the two areas are very different from each other. Even after four decades of living in Fujian, Grandma could not pronounce the word *xi* or death. Instead, she said *chee* in a thick Yunnan accent. *"Wo yao ga moh chee qu lor!"* or "I'm hungry to death!" was her favorite refrain in the Hokkien dialect. Then she would fry some rice and wolf it down.

She put leftover fried rice on the kitchen table for Younger Sister and me to eat after school. Flies buzzed over our dinner, and the pork fat in the cooked rice congealed, causing us to lose our appetites.

Grandma was never concerned. With her bird-like eyes, big flat face, and thin lips, she was not the affectionate type. Yet, Grandma was unpretentious and displayed no favoritism. She was the first person to treat Younger Sister and me as equals.

Grandma made it clear to us right at the beginning that we were not to disturb her life too much or bother her with our emotional needs. Whenever we missed our family and got teary, she refused to have any of it and just walked away.

Grandma carried a heavy bunch of keys that hung around her waist because her habit was to lock everything valuable in the cabinets inside her master room.

When Grandma was a young girl, she attempted foot-binding to increase her chances of marrying upwards. But the binding failed. Nonetheless, her feet were half-destroyed.

Her bulky body protested above her broken feet whenever she hastened her pace. She swayed exaggeratedly from side to side and looked like she could topple over at any second.

Then her keys would jingle loudly. The noise and the clumsy movements saddened me.

I empathized with Grandma.

At the same time, seeing her fleeing left me wondering what scared Grandma most: handling our emotions or showing hers.

Amid the sorrows of being left behind and living in the lonely Leung Mansion, a joyous thing happened.

I encountered and fell in love with Chinese literature.

The Four Great Chinese Novels – *Water Margin, Romance of the Three Kingdoms, Journey to the West,* and *Dream of the Red Chamber* – became my soothing, stimulating companions.

Depictions of these novels' scenes were painted on the mansion's inner walls and carved onto the stone pillars and window frames. They created a surreal environment in which I could hide, seek, and dream.

I imagined other worlds that existed in a different time and space.

Gazing at those paintings and carvings, I forgot where or who I was.

It was such a relief – to be free from one's slight yet heavy self.

I began to read the simplified versions of these marvelous novels. Then, I started a lifetime passion for *Dream of the Red Chamber*.

The book featured three protagonists – Baoyu, Daiyu, and Baochai. Baoyu, the central character, was the reincarnation of a sentient and quasi-anthropomorphic stone. Daiyu's previous life was a plant, and in their former lives, they met.

One of the main plots was about the triangular love affair between the three. But that did not fascinate me then. It was the personalities of these three protagonists that enthralled me.

Baoyu's fear of his father drew me close to him. And I liked that everyone loved him, except for his father. Baoyu was handsome, kind, and generous, especially toward marginalized people.

Baochai was sensible and tactful. Her healthy look and boyish demeanor attracted me.

But it was the unconventional and hypersensitive Daiyu who charmed me the most.

Daiyu's mother died. She moved to live with her matriarch, maternal grandmother – Baoyu's paternal grandmother – in Rongguo House.

The house was a massive mansion for the large, rich, and famous Jia Family.

Daiyu started living in the outlandish Rongguo House when she was nine. Upon learning this, the similarity of our fates struck me.

Daiyu and I both came to live in a monstrous mansion, among many strange, scary relatives, at a similarly young age – she was nine, I was ten.

Instantly, Daiyu became my friend. We struggled together.

And when Daiyu cried, which was frequently, she permitted me to weep, too.

A depiction in the corner of a wall in the upper hall featured Daiyu alone in the Grand View Garden inside the Rongguo House, resembling a Garden of Eden for the teenage protagonists. The picture portrayed the fragile Daiyu gathering and burying the fallen flower petals.

Whenever I felt like crying, I would sit next to a stone pillar at the back of the grand hall, behind the altar. Looking out from the dark corner and up to the wall, I had an unimpeded view of Daiyu's depiction in a flower-burying scene.

The hidden corner became my refuge – the safe spot to sit and spend time with Daiyu alone. The stout stone pillar in the front hall concealed me completely. The privacy provided idyllic surroundings for my sorrow to meet Daiyu's.

Gradually, the fragrance of the petals, the earth, and the grasses combined with Daiyu's water-lily-like perfume transformed the air around me. Such serene scents soon dispersed my melancholy.

Then, I shifted my attention to the poem inscribed in the upper right corner of the depiction. It was entitled *Lin Daiyu's Elegy on Flowers*.

The first two couplets (translated by Hawkes) read as follows.

> The blossoms fade and falling fill the air
> Of fragrance and bright hues bereft and bare
> Floss drifts and flutters around the Maiden's bower
> Or softly strikes against her curtained door.

Though I did not understand the poem, I would murmur some of its words and phrases. They sounded musical and consolatory and echoed beautifully inside my mind.

The beauty of the scene, its depiction, and the inscription entranced me. The stone pillar supported my back nicely, even as its chillness sent ripples through my body.

*

I was nicknamed *Wouling*, Dark Ling, because of my dark complexion.

Relatives and friends of my parents understood that I was the least favorite child.

Many adults tended to be extra nice to the favorable one – Younger Sister – to please my parents. Those adults chose to ignore me.

Previously, my mother complimented Younger Sister on her talents in front of our relatives whenever we returned to Nan'an to celebrate Chinese New Year.

Younger Sister sang and danced during these family gatherings. The relatives clapped and cheered for her. She was the center of attention while I was her shadow.

But now, after the departure of my parents and elder siblings to Hong Kong, my younger sister suddenly lost her halo. I thought it would please me to see her descend to my level. But it was not so.

Every time I stole a surreptitious glance at Younger Sister, the misery in her eyes made me feel like drowning. Quickly, I looked away to stop my heart from aching.

But I could not let her know that I pitied her. I was afraid it would sadden her more because I was her despondent *Leegi,* or Second Elder Sister, as she called me.

So, I tried to keep my distance.

But like lychees with thin skin, Younger Sister was vulnerable. Her eyes had oblivion, distraction, and fragility written all through them.

I wanted to give her shelter and hope. But I had none to offer. It tortured me to stay near or away from her, and the two notions repeatedly tore at my heart. It made me feel so lost, weary, and vanquished.

Sometimes, Younger Sister and I would play with our cousins in the monstrous mansion. My second uncle's two sons' ages were closest to us, so we often played together.

Second Uncle was square-faced and small-eyed like Grandma.

He was medium-built and pale. As he had difficulty finding a job, Grandpa gave him some money to run a grocery store next to the mansion.

But the uncle often left his wife managing the shop. He regularly returned to the house to sleep during the day and went out at night to drink and gamble with other villagers.

Whenever the four of us argued, Second Uncle would run out of his room and yell at my younger sister and me. He accused the two of us of being troublemakers.

The uncle's two sons, my cousins, were not evil; they played civilly with us.

But after a couple of instances of their father supporting them when they were in the wrong, they became meaner. The conflicts that we could have easily solved between us before would escalate quickly into fights.

One day, when we were having one of those nasty arguments, my second uncle rushed out of his room. Without a word, he came to me.

Stretching out his hand, he tried to grab hold of my arm. I ran.

He turned to my younger sister instead.

The minute she saw him coming at her, she stood stock-still. Her eyes and mouth were agape, and her body quivered.

I wanted to shout and tell her to run. But I did not. I feared it would make Second Uncle come back at me. I ran further and hid behind a stone pillar in the front part of the grand hall.

A bit later, when I could breathe better, I looked back from the pillar.

The uncle clamped his iron fingers around the wrist of my younger sister as if he meant to squeeze it off. His free hand pointed toward his room, and he asked his son to get a feather duster. His elder son did so.

Once Second Uncle got the duster, he told my younger sister to bend forward. He began to thrash her bottom hard with the duster handle. Once. Twice. Three times.

As he continued beating her, he yelled:

"I asked you to stop fighting with my sons. You never listen, do you? Do you? See if this can help you listen!"

His sons laughed. But they stopped when they saw their father incessantly whipping my younger sister. It shocked them too. And it stunned them when they realized my younger sister did not make a sound.

Younger Sister must have been surprised at such a savage act as she went slack, nearly doubled up. Her bottom was a deflated football.

She appeared to be paralyzed with despair.

No crying. No resistance.

Tears rushed down my cheeks and splashed onto the tiles.

I pushed my knuckles hard into my eyes to stop myself from crying.

Younger Sister's silence terrified the uncle. He stopped, giving her a quick look. Then he let go of her and returned to his room with his sons.

Younger Sister fell onto the floor.

My mind urged me to run to her, but my feet would not move. Like a trail of thick snot, my body stuck to the pillar.

The night that followed was long and tortured.

As I was afraid of the dark, I usually kept the two halves of the door slightly ajar. And I put a high-backed wooden armchair, the heaviest chair I could find in the house, behind the door, just in case.

Our room was next to the open courtyard in the center of the house. A solitary shaft of moonlight seeped through the gap between the doors and silvered the room.

I sat up in bed and stared at the back of Younger Sister.

She was asleep facing the wall. She turned around; I looked away. She stayed turned in for a minute or two, then out again. Her breathing was shallow. Then I heard sobbing sounds and quickly looked at her face. Her eyes were closed as if she was still asleep.

Drawing up my legs, I encircled my arms around my knees, rested my head on them, and listened to her sobs, feeling my heart ache with every sound.

Sometime later, the sound of her sobbing faded, and her breathing deepened. She became stiller and stayed facing out. I raised my head, put down my legs, and turned to face her. My heart tightened, and my back ached. A cold feeling clenched me.

Younger Sister's face, chubby with baby fat, was cute in its misery. Her lips pursed in discomfort, and her brow furrowed in sadness. A few strands of faintly misty hair stuck to her left cheek. I stroked them away. Tear stains, the fresh and wet ones, below her eyes gleamed in the dimness of the night.

My eyes fixed on her tear stains. Then, my attention moved to her pillow. It dawned on me that the cushion might also be tear-stained. I wished to remove the pad and let her pillow be my arm.

After a while, I reached out to take her hand resting on her right leg. Then, I saw the deep violet and blue marks on her wrists.

Sitting upright, I gasped at her bruises. They stabbed at my heart, pulling me apart. And it felt like the stone pillar was falling on me, crushing me to pieces.

I heard a strange, shaky voice coming from the back of my throat murmuring to her:

"I'm so sorry, Younger Sister. Your *Leegi* is so useless."

The voice continued wailing:

"She is a coward and didn't even try to protect you!"

Two weeks after my younger sister was beaten, there was a movie screening. In those days in Nan'an, the only opportunity to watch a movie was when a rich man returned from overseas.

To celebrate his *yi jin huan xiang* [homecoming in glory] his family would hire the community film crew to show a movie in an open area, usually on a threshing ground.

The crew members hung a white cloth screen up on a wall. They put a projector close to the screen, and someone standing next to it ran the reel by hand.

That night, I brought a low wooden chair and went with others to watch it.

The movie was about the brave Chinese Eighth Route Army fighting off the ruthless imperial Japanese invaders. It was pretty much the only type of film we could see then.

Some time into the movie, I suddenly felt something warm and wet running down my trousers. I realized it was my pee – what was wrong with me?

I grabbed my chair and snuck away.

Forgetting my fear of the dark and field animals, I hurried through the ebony trails among rice paddy fields and headed home.

Once I arrived, I shut the door, tightened it, and leaned on it to catch my breath.

I removed my trousers and panties in disgust. Together with the short wooden chair, I shoved them all underneath the bed.

The thought of them, the fear that something was wrong with me, and the ultimate feeling of shame – of being a filthy, useless person – kept me up all night.

When I heard the cock's first crow, I jumped off the bed, retrieved the three items, and hastened out of the room.

It was still dark outside. I went to the kitchen and got a half-used bar of brown soap and an enamel washbasin. I held the basin with clothes and soap in one hand and a small chair in another, rushing to the washing area around the well.

A bucket with a rope tied to it stood next to the short wall built around the well's mouth. I dropped the bucket into the darkness, holding the line. Leaning over the deep hole, with the faintest hint of warmer air rising against my face, I hauled the bucket hand over hand until it rose suddenly into view, the dim sky shimmering within like some luminous oil.

I poured the water into the wash basin over my disgusting clothes. The iciness of the water cut through my hands' thin skin, and my fingers recoiled instantly. But I gritted my teeth, grasped the clothes, and rubbed them hard.

Then, I applied a bit of soap and continued to scrub them. I could not use too much soap. Grandma would notice and scold me for being wasteful. Or worse, she might discover this shameful incident of mine.

I did not know what this incident was, why it happened, or whether it would persist or disappear; I had no idea.

I locked the fears and anger all within myself. I did not want to tell anyone or let anyone find out. They would despise me even more. The thought terrified me.

I found a small, sharp stone, scoured and scrubbed and rubbed and wiped at the clothes. The skin of my hands threatened to peel off. Every time I changed the water, I poured the used liquid over the chair to wash it.

After what felt like a million times, I squeezed the water out of the clothes. Every molecule of my body screamed when I tried to stand straight. Hanging the clothes up, I hid them among the rest of the laundry.

A day passed, and no one noticed it. I was relieved.

But for a long time, I smelled the stink of urine around me all the time.

And then, another thing occurred. It happened to the area around the middle of the right side of my neck. It started to swell up and grew into the size of a rice dumpling, repugnant and horrifying.

I showed the problem to Grandma, who glanced at it and went into her room.

A few minutes later, she returned and handed me a small jar with medicine powder. It was her famous hometown remedy, the Yunnan White Medicine.

Grandma asked me to mix the medicine with water and drink it. She said I ate too many lychees, which produced too much *yang* or fire. She told me the remedy was *yin* and would cool off the fire, and then I would be alright.

The situation worsened as the ball grew bigger, filthier, and redder. It threatened to burst.

Reluctantly, Grandma took me to a doctor, who scheduled a minor surgery the next day and removed the abscess. I took some antibiotics and wore a patch over the wound.

Every two days, I returned to the clinic alone and got the injury adequately cleaned and the patch renewed.

One day, instead of the nurse, the doctor cleared the patch and cleaned the wound for me. He inspected it closely and declared that the infection was gone.

When I arrived home and looked in the mirror, there was a distinct blemish over that place on my neck. It was bumpy to the touch. I have the scar to this day.

Luckily, the school was heaven for my younger sister and me.

Coming from a respectable family, we were highly regarded, special ones. Furthermore, we had returned from other places, places unfamiliar to the other kids in school. We were the envy of other students. Many had never traveled or even stepped out of the village. We were doubly admirable as we had been traveling between our parents' working places and Nan'an every year or two.

We soon attracted our respective followers and went about our lives separately in school.

I was in a trio of good girlfriends, and a boy trailed along after us. The four of us often played hopscotch or rope skipping during recess. For some reason, I always got an additional chance to play the game if I lost early.

After school, we would visit each other's homes, except mine, because nobody and no snack awaited us. On the other hand, my friends' mothers welcomed my visits. So I usually went to my friends' homes and lingered there.

My friends' mothers would treat me to *loufai* or *mouhzhou* – two kinds of Nan'an sweet snacks. Their ingredients included wheat flour, vegetable oil, egg, milk, granulated sugar, and malt sugar, with *loufai* white due to its crisp rice coat and *mouhzhou* earthy brown with roasted peanuts. Being crisper, *loufai* was the preferred choice for the children.

But I wasn't crazy about either *loufai* or *mouhzhou* as I did not have a sweet tooth. Or rather, sweet did not seem to have a place in my life.

Sometimes, my friends' mothers would go further and make me savory scallion crepes – my favorite. The freshly made scallion crepes carried an intoxicating aroma. Their mildly burned, crispy edges were divine.

Often, I picked off a corner of the crepe and put it deliberately into my mouth, chewing it for a long, long time before I let it go and swallowed. The grease that remained inside my mouth felt so velvety and comforting. It obliterated whatever acrimonious aftertaste I sensed at the back of my throat before. And more amazingly, when the fabulous fragrance of the caramelized scallion filled my mouth and nostrils, the smell of home, motherly love, and care would wrap softly around me.

I wished to bottle such a heartwarming scent and savor it over and over again.

I enrolled in Nan'an in the second half of Primary 4 and went on to Primary 5 and 6. I performed well in general. Then, lychees seemed to bring out a unique fire in me. I excelled in Chinese.

My Chinese teacher, Teacher Li, was in his early fifties and slim. Being six feet tall, he stood out, towering over other teachers.

Also, Teacher Li reminded me of the renowned writer Lu Xun, whom my mother revered. Like Lu, he had a thick mustache and a pair of dense eyebrows often locked together, giving him a stern, fearsome look.

Teacher Li enabled me to taste the elixir of triumph, the first taste of it in my life.

Every week, we had to submit a composition. Teacher Li paid great attention to our work. When it was time to return the pieces to us with his comments, he often kept mine. He read my compositions out loud in front of the class. It frequently happened during the two and a half years that I studied with him.

The image of his first reading of my composition is burned wondrously into my memory.

There were four rows in our classroom. I sat in the front seat of the second row from the door. Teacher Li stood next to my chair when he read my composition. He held the piece of paper with my extensive, strong handwriting as if he were clasping a precious stone full of tenderness and appreciation.

Teacher Li stood elegantly with his long, straight legs together. As he read, his body swayed slightly forward and backward in sync with the rhythm of his reading. When he encountered a verb used ingeniously or a beautiful phrase, his forward movements extended further, and he was on his toes for a second or two. Then he gracefully landed back on his heels and launched into another round of gentle rocking.

When he finished the reading, his thick eyebrows parted, and his mouth widened. An approving, transfiguring smile blossomed on his wise, wrinkled face.

Teacher Li turned to me and said:

"Young lady, you can certainly write."

A delicious shiver of excitement ran through my body. The teacher's smile and words became a surge of energy that enveloped me. It felt like bathing in the early morning sun, and such a gentle sun gradually warmed my heart and brought a glorious glow to my cheeks.

The experience lifted the weight of self-hatred from my stiff neck, tight shoulders, and sore back. I sat upright.

Some of my classmates looked admiringly at me. I received their silent praises with grace – a virtue I did not know existed within me before that moment.

I wished to bottle that moment – the moment of recognition and triumph – and show it to my father and mother.

And I wanted to tell my parents: "*Ba, Ma,* look! Your *Wou Ling* isn't so useless!"

*

When I discovered my writing talent, I began to write to my mother.

Upon finishing the first letter, I folded it neatly, gave it to Grandma, and asked her to help post it for me. But after I had written about four letters over the next three months, no reply came. Getting suspicious and anxious, I checked with Grandma again. She told me she gave the letters to my second uncle because he was the one who went to the market to purchase products for his shop and he had a better chance of posting them.

It was highly likely that Second Uncle read my letters and destroyed them because I mentioned he had hit my younger sister in one of those letters.

I rewrote a new long one that summarized the last four and kept it inside my school bag. When I visited a friend one day, I asked her mother to help post it. She agreed.

About two weeks later, Grandma gave me her signature hateful, stern look that something was up when I returned from school. I wondered what I had done this time to annoy her. She came close to me and retrieved something from the pocket of her trousers. It was a letter. She handed it to me.

I was electrified and thought I must be dreaming. I kept staring at the letter and forgot to breathe. Then astonishment gave way to glee. I received the letter from Grandma, thanked her, and broke into a run.

I ran to my usual spot next to the stone pillar behind the altar as fast as possible. Sitting down, I held the letter close to my throbbing chest and took a few deep breaths to calm myself.

Looking out, I saw the sun weaving its golden threads together and making a large, thin bamboo sieve in the courtyard. A few sparrows flew in, landed charmingly on the roof beams, and chirped away gaily. I looked up at the wall and caught Daiyu's ephemeral smile.

Beholding my mother's letter for a long moment, I unfolded it. Her tame, elegant handwriting jumped into my eyes:

"My dearest Ling and Ting, you are the treasures of my life."

Tears streamed in rivulets down my cheeks.

Mother said she was beyond herself when she received my letter. She mentioned that she had written to Grandma many times asking about us. But Grandma just replied that all was well. Nothing special. Finally, receiving my letter gave her bliss and misery at once.

Mother was delighted to reconnect with us and stricken to learn about our deplorable situation. She promised to do everything she could to improve our living conditions.

She assured us that she had written to tell Grandma she would send her more monthly money and asked her to hire a part-time helper to cook dinner for us. She appealed to Grandma to ensure we would have at least one hot meal a day.

Furthermore, she had Father write a severe letter to my uncle asking him never to lay a hand on us ever again.

I sprang from my seat with joy.

The sense of achievement filled my body with strength and hope.

It made me realize that being me was not always wrong or terrible, after all.

I bottled the moment.

Soon, I ran looking for my younger sister. Once I found her, I took her to the courtyard.

Late afternoon sunlight bedecked the yard. The upper grand hall was about two steps higher than the yard. I sat her on the stone edge of the grand lobby. Her legs dangled above the warm, sunlit ground. I showed her the letter and gave her a quick summary:

"Mother did not forget about us; she loved and missed us very much!"

Tears flooded her eyes.

I went on quickly:

"No, we had not done anything wrong, and they did not abandon us."

I breathed and almost shouted out in delight:

"We were not unwanted!"

Big teardrops rolled down her cheeks.

"Our lives will be much better from now on because Mother will back us up."

Younger Sister stared at me, disbelieving. She turned to the letter, touched it, smelled it, placed it against her chest, held it in front of her, read it, and reread it.

She whispered a few words and phrases under her breath. Her tears were drying.

Slowly, she looked up and regarded me with happiness, appreciation, and admiration.

"*Leegi*," she called, leaped off her seat, and reached out to me.

We hugged. We cried. We laughed. We shouted. We danced.

Hahaha! The peals of our laughter intertwined and filled the courtyard.

Grandma was angry and ignored me for a month.

Then, when I returned from school one day, she asked if I was hungry. If her face had not been so comical, I would have probably cried. She had received an increased allowance from my mother.

Grandma hired a widow next door, an old lady, to help out. However, she did not allow the helper to cook because she was afraid the woman would use too much oil or steal her food. So, Grandma prepared some dinner for us by herself.

As for Second Uncle, he hated me.

But the uncle did not dare to hit or even scold me again.

Instead, he resorted to giving me scornful looks. Whenever he saw that I was coming his way, he would stare at me so hard and for so long, ensuring that I noticed the loathing look in his eyes before letting me pass.

Those were very unpleasant experiences, but his looks did not hurt me.

Even then, I felt sorry for him. Because I had been my younger sister's shadow, I understood this uncle well. It must not have been easy for him to grow up in the eclipse of my bright, tyrannical father all his life.

But I also knew it was wrong of him to revenge himself on us.

I kept Younger Sister and myself away from Second Uncle.

As a result, my writing directly improved my life and my younger sister's.

The mail between my mother and I continued. This period of correspondence was my closest and most precious time with my mother.

Also, inherited from my mother, I had a pleasant voice.

After the initial music classes, our music teacher noticed my singing aptitude and selected me to attend the annual prefectural inter-school singing contest.

Our school vice-headmaster was an excellent player of the *erhu,* or the two-stringed fiddle. So our music teacher invited him to play his *erhu,* accompanying my singing. He gladly accepted. We started practicing straight away, three times a week after school.

On the morning of the singing contest, he rode his bicycle to pick me up from my home as it was a Saturday.

When I sat tight on the back of his deep-green bike, he handed me his *erhu* to hold onto, and we went on our way to the town hall to attend the competition.

I lost after the first round.

When we came out of the hall, hefty, chunky clouds covered the sky, and the sun hid behind the clouds.

The vice-headmaster and I got back on his bike. I put his *erhu* on my lap, grasped its handle with one hand, and the other held onto his waist.

He rode on steadily and often turned back to check on me.

Sometimes, he gave me a quick grin. He even joked a little and thanked me for allowing him to pick up his beloved instrument again.

I smiled back and held on tightly to his *erhu.*

A sense of security shrouded me – the security of knowing that people would still care about me and like me even if I failed.

Lightheartedly, I turned my attention to the heavens.

Some of the clouds got thinner; some drifted to join others.

There were bulky bushes and feathery snowflakes. Massive mushrooms moved toward us – ever-changing and entrancing. My eyes dashed amidst the kaleidoscopic patterns of the clouds.

Suddenly, the sun emerged.

Its striking shafts of light fell on the land and transformed it.

A deep, delicious peace came upon me.

Maybe it was possible to live on like this – without my parents – and be happy.

Part Three: Darkness

Hong Kong

1989 – 1990

Form 1 Fairy

It was September 1989.

The sexual assault had happened six months ago.

I got into a prestigious Government English secondary school.

When Form 1 started, I had to walk for half an hour to get to the bus stop, and it took about forty minutes to arrive at the new school.

I did not mind commuting for over an hour each morning – the further away from home, the better.

I stopped seeing Coach.

I stopped visiting the youth center.

I stopped playing table tennis altogether.

My menstruation had come for the first time in the spring of that year, about one or two months before the rape.

It was a late afternoon. After using our toilet strip, I got up, discovered so much blood, and nearly screamed. I thought I had urinated blood.

Mother happened to be home. She chuckled, called me a silly girl (which I found endearing), and told me to keep quiet and wait for her. She came in, handed me a sanitary pad, and showed me how to put it on.

I was very grateful to her and wondered how motherless girls handled it. I felt really sorry for them.

But now, I could not tell Mother what had happened with Coach. It was too shameful.

For the first time in my life, I did not want her attention.

*

My body shape began to change, making me feel like a little woman.

But my classmates were two years younger; they seemed childlike and carefree.

I grew my hair long, and my appearance improved. During school assemblies, I overheard some whispers and realized that some students called me the "Form 1 fairy."

From time to time, older boys from senior forms came to my floor to check on me through our classroom windows.

But the attention did not bring me joy or glory. On the contrary, I wished to go underground unnoticed.

It was because I saw myself as awkward and exposed, like a snail that lost its hard round shell. With its unpleasantly soft body, the shell-less snail crept around or perched on the edge of the chair.

Like my younger self who experienced the incontinence incident, I tried to bury deep inside me this "thing" that happened with Coach.

But such things became like stones that got into the pocket of my new light blue school dress; they jiggled loud and clear in my head when I walked.

Still, I did not tell my parents, family, or girlfriends about what had occurred.

Form-1-me often bought a loaf of raisin or milk-and-butter bread and had it for breakfast and lunch. This way, I could stay alone in the classroom during recess or lunch break. I would stand by the last window at the end of the room, gaze out, and nibble on my bread.

Sometimes, my eyes would turn misty for no reason.

The secondary school sat atop a steep slope. Our Form 1 classroom on the second floor was already relatively high above the surroundings. The view outside the window was bleak – mostly the boring matchbox-like high-rises of Hong Kong under a desolate sky.

The days were emptiness – a vast emptiness in which being alive became almost meaningless. Such bareness, like a powerful vacuum cleaner, sucked out the supposedly exciting new secondary school life.

The silence, and the featureless autumn sky of Hong Kong, remained.

The inescapable fact that everything around me was monotonous, that in terms of tables and chairs and blackboard, I did not exist. These things rendered me invisible, even to myself.

I was not conscious of what was happening.

I lived it.

I became invisible.

I lost myself.

Our class teacher, Ms. Ng, was also our art teacher. "Art" refers to drawing. If there was one thing I absolutely could not do well in my life, it had to be drawing.

When I was in Primary 5 and 6 in my parents' hometown, Nan'an, I would do written compositions for good girlfriends and ask them to paint for me. I could not draw, and so far, I had managed to survive the art classes without getting unnecessary attention.

However, there was no way to shun embarrassment this time.

Ms. Ng was a uniquely dressed, petite woman who carried an air of chicness and confidence.

She had shoulder-length hair, usually wore navy blue or deep color skirts, and tied various hues of scarves around her neck.

Ms. Ng was determined to persuade me that everyone could paint if they tried.

When we sketched a still object during class, Ms. Ng often came to stand behind me and observed for some time. I perspired so much in a cold, air-conditioned room.

My hands shook so badly that I dropped the pencil often. Once I got sick, I excused myself, ran to the toilet, and vomited.

The skinny me became smaller in front of Ms. Ng.

The tiger in me ceased to exist, and the rabbit in me got panicky and tearful fast.

My strangeness kept the schoolmates away. The distance and isolation suited me.

Alone in the classroom during recess, sometimes I would throw little pieces of paper outside the window to watch the breeze whisk them away, imagining myself floating down after them and wondering if I would also land unharmed on the sidewalk.

On sunny days, I fantasized about finding a way to get to the rooftop and sliding down the shaft of light, holding the frictionless beam in my hands.

And then, I started stealing.

I stole two of my father's cigarettes.

The night after I took them, I found a lighter and kept all these inside my pocket. After midnight, I sneaked out of our hut, walked a short distance away, and sat in a corner.

The malodorous drainage ditch next to me was revolting. I quickly retrieved the lighter, took out a cigarette, and held it between my lips like my father did. I lit it. A little corner of it caught fire. I sucked hard at it and almost choked to death.

When the cough finally dwindled, a terrible taste of bitterness stuck at the back of my throat. The cigarette dropped into the ditch during my violent coughing.

I took out the other cigarette, put it between my lips, and lit it. After sucking in a little, the cigarette end began glowing in the darkness. I pushed the red burning top into my flesh near my left wrist.

One Sunday afternoon, as I was ironing my school dress, I launched the iron tip into the inner skin of my lower arm. A skin strip, two fingers wide, burned, and its edges quickly curled.

I removed the iron tip and felt the pain peak.

Closing my eyes, I let the pain's sharpness cut through my body.

For a second or two or three, the pain helped captivate the cacophony in my head.

The cacophony consisted of screams like these, day and night:

It's your fault! It's your fault! It's your fault!
You are filthy! You are disgusting!
You are good for nothing!
Even your parents can't stand you!

Whenever I lay wide awake at night, Coach's eyes approached.

His hands were all over me again.

The feelings that followed made me forget how to be brave, how to be confident, how to be daring, how to be polite, how to be sensitive, how to be caring, and how to be myself.

Could I ever return to my parents' hometown, enter Leung's Mansion, raise my head high, and look my great-grandpa in the eye again? No, I could not.

Anger, terror, shame, confusion, and irritation were creamed together in my head.

I wanted to scream but found neither strength nor voice.

Physical and mental exhaustion apprehended me.

But I could not sleep.

My mind would not slow down, would not rest.

I banged my fist or my head sometimes against the wall.

My family did not notice anything wrong with me.

Was I so good at hiding my emotions now?

Or were they simply ignoring me?

Maybe a bit of both.

When Ms. Ng finally had enough of my silence, detachment, and other unusual behavior, she referred me to the school's social worker.

The social worker's office was in an awkward corner between two floors, and I had difficulty finding it the first time. I took the stairs up and down the two floors many times and never realized there was an office between them. When I saw it, I knocked on the door.

"Come in." A light, lovely voice came out.

I turned the handle and opened the door.

"Please come in and close the door behind you."

Dragging my feet, I did as I was told.

"You're Fongling, right? I'm Judith. It's nice meeting you."

Judith smiled up at me. Her body filled the armchair.

I kept my head low and murmured something in reply.

She looked to be in her late twenties, perhaps freshly out of graduate school.

"Come, sit down here."

She pointed to the chair next to her table.

My eyes scanned the narrow strip of her office.

It reminded me of the kitchen/toilet in our hut.

Her desk faced the wall. A filing cabinet and a messily encumbered bookshelf stood behind her chair. The gray walls felt like the rest of the school, lifeless.

I shifted a small step forward and sat on the edge of the armless chair.

She searched for my eyes and asked:

"How is your day going?"

"Okay, thanks."

"How are your classes?"

"They are okay."

"And your classmates?"

"They are fine too. Thanks."

My head lowered further, trying to avoid her eyes the whole time.

She smiled, pushed back her chair, stood up, turned to the filing cabinet, and opened it.

Piles of old files were there; some slid down and fell.

She shoved them back, took a file from the top shelf, and shut the cabinet's doors.

Her eyes swept through a document in the file when she sat back down.

It was probably an evaluation form, as Ms. Ng's signature appeared.

She looked at me again and asked gently:

"Is there anything you would like to talk about?"

"No, not really."

We dragged on for about an hour.

When she finally told me that my time was up, I almost breathed a sigh of relief.

As I got up to leave, the books looked as if they were about to slide off the shelf and knock me down.

Coming out of her room, I trudged for a while and reached the end of a corridor.

A blue balustrade was in front of me.

I leaned forward and rested my elbows on the rail, gazing into space.

A crooked road stretched endlessly toward the horizon.

The wind ceased.

The dust smelled of dead leaves and flowers.

Death seemed peaceful; life dull, purposeless.

The mournful cry of a fledgling broke out and filled the air.

The early evening was ending as it got darker and darker.

A little blackbird flew by and settled on the far end of the rail.

Fearless or hurt, it turned its beak up.

It looked as if the small blackbird was challenging the big sky.

And by looking up, perhaps it felt as enormous as the heavens for a change.

The Diary

One day after school, I got off the bus at Rainbow Village, one stop earlier than usual, taking a walk home.

Rainbow Village was a government low-cost housing estate close to our slum.

I was walking along the village's periphery in my usual somnambulist state, not taking in anything, but when I reached a street corner, a stationery shop caught my attention.

I went toward the shop and stopped in front of its display window, taking an idle look at the objects. Piled about was a mélange of stationery. Nothing special. I was soon bored.

When I was about to turn and resume my sleepwalking, something attracted me.

It was a diary.

With its soft and thick covers, it looked like a safe box. It had a lock and a key attached, albeit the set appeared more decorative than real. Still, the diary was exquisite.

The front cover featured a beautiful blonde young lady with her long, loose, wavy hair falling nicely on her back. She was propping her chin, deep in some thoughts.

The melancholic elements in the girl's eyes reminded me of my close childhood friend – Daiyu – one of the protagonists in *Dream of the Red Chamber*.

I hurried into the shop and asked the man behind the counter to show the diary to me.

When the diary first landed in my hands, I felt it belonged to me. I could never let it go.

Quickly, I asked for the price. It was expensive.

Luckily, I found enough money in my pocket because I had not been spending much on breakfast and lunch, as I usually only had a loaf of bread to cover the two meals.

I immediately bought the diary.

Upon arriving home, I changed into shorts, climbed to my upper bunk bed, and wanted to start writing.

My mind went blank. I did not know what to write.

Grudgingly, I put the diary down.

But I could not take my eyes off my "safebox."

For some reason, I believed writing possessed magical powers that could save and revive.

I recalled the eleven-, twelve-year-old me in Fujian who wrote letters to my mother in Hong Kong and improved my and my younger sister's lives.

Writing had empowered me once. It brought on profound changes.

So now, if I unloaded the tormenting things in my head and heart into this new safebox, they could become manageable.

I might be able to find my voice and myself through writing.

The thoughts propelled me. I tried hard to write during the following weeks.

A few broken passages with fragmented phrases began to emerge in my diary.

These early phrases were airy and sentimental.

Then, I made my initial attempt at composing a *ci*, or lyric poem.

My first Chinese *ci* was born:

Elegy on Spring
Dreary drizzles of spring keep descending
Pitiable petals of flowers continue falling

Is it the descending drizzles triggering the petals to fall
Or the falling petals prompting the drizzle to descend?

The heavens remain aloof and distant
And let a silent song seal the earth

It is the silent song of spring
Lamenting its irretrievable losses

Then, another *ci* rushed out of me:

Swallow and Sorrow
You are a wounded swallow
Still, you try to fly, to fly out of your sorrows
But your sorrows cling to you
Then they take over every inch of your being

Weary and depressed
Where can you rest?
Where can you become invisible?
To stay quiet. Not to be disturbed.

The same old feathers, the same old sky
Though your feelings and thoughts differ from those of the
bygone times
Raindrops hasten the falling flowers
You shake and shake and shake so hard to try and shake off the
sorrows

They cling and cling and cling so hard onto you
And like the swallows, they always return
In groups, outside your eaves
And sing their songs non-stop.
Unstoppable.

I began writing paragraphs about my daily encounters, thoughts, and feelings.

The writing became more comprehensible.

And the most wondrous thing was that when I was writing in my upper bunk bed, even if the rest of the family was around, I felt alone and peaceful.

When I wrote, I fell into a trance – feeling blissful.

The damaged shell of a snail was growing back, albeit at a gentle pace.

A slight yet appreciative or even satisfactory smile returned to my face from time to time.

I kept the diary beside my pillow and touched it often.

Sometimes, I even held it close to my chest.

Having it close to me helped me sleep.

Even if sleep would not come, I did not feel so bad as before because I had my diary – something that captured some original parts of me and was piecing them together, one by one, ever so slowly, so tenderly.

One day, I pulled open the rusty iron gate when I arrived home.

Guang! The gate seemed to groan louder than usual.

I descended the two steps.

Brother sat in front of the TV like he did most of the time, losing himself in the cartoons.

As soon as he saw me walking down, he threw a huge smile at me.

My body shivered. Gingerly, I approached my bed.

Bit by bit, I climbed to my upper bunk.

My diary was gone!

I nearly fell on my back to the ground.

Quickly, I grabbed hold of an iron rung and steadied myself.

A second or two later, I managed to scramble up to my upper bunk and sat on its edge.

Hehe. My brother laughed. He raised my diary and yelled:

"Yeah, our writer is home now! Let's have a reading of her great work!"

Mother popped her head out of the kitchen.

Haha. Mother laughed with Brother.

I froze and stared at them in disbelief.

Deliberately and extravagantly, he opened the cover of my diary.

Kum! Kum! He cleared his throat.

And he started to read aloud the contents of my diary:

"…"

I looked at his mouth, his laugh, his gestures.

And then, it felt like Coach was all over me again.

That night, I took the diary and went out of the hut.

A light rain had been falling for a while.

I ran to the playground and hid underneath the bumpy old table-tennis table.

Then I started tearing the diary apart, a couple of pages at a time, into pieces.

Arranging the shreds into a bundle inside the hardcovers, I took out a lighter and lit it.

It flared and lit up my face.

I found a stick that looked like a three-pronged fork and turned the bits with it.

The burning stopped a couple of times because of the damp air and the gusty winds.

I relit them time and again.

The paper shreds had gone to ashes.

Only the hardcovers and binding remained.

I folded the covers as if the leaves were still intact.

Then I cradled the whole thing, a sacred remnant, in my palms.

Inch by inch, I moved from under the table.

I picked up a stone with sharp edges that fitted my hand.

Gripping the stone, I went to a clammy corner of a grimy wall and began digging.

I dug a hole and buried the remains of my diary in it.

A sense of exhaustion engulfed me.

I slumped onto the ground above my diary's grave.

The rain was falling with disheartening steadiness.

Such solemn stillness, joined with an unsettling quietness, somehow brought Daiyu back to my mind. She cut and burned all Baoyu's letters and poems to her before she died when she was fifteen, about the same age as me then.

The Moon in a Dog's Eye

The summer of 1990 came, closing the first year of my secondary school life.

The once sky-lit room in my heart had disappeared. The hopeful, hardworking me felt like light-years away.

Instead, a dark, cold cell captured my thoughts and feelings.

I could not reach out. I could not cry. I could not sleep. I could not dream anymore.

One night in the wee hours, I gazed at the moonlight that slid gracefully through the rusty iron gate of our hut. Her gentle light transformed the entrance and the steps beyond it, giving them a magical glow.

The moon's sense of serenity allured me. It generated an urge in me to join her in the peaceful world out there beneath its gleam.

The rest of my family was sound asleep. Creeping down from my upper bunk bed, I quietly unlocked the gate and walked away. My flip-flops were stardust, carrying me away from our home.

Weaving through the narrow winding paths of our slum, I hurried toward a nearby construction site at Tate's Cairn Tunnel in Diamond Hill.

I needed space, a quiet place where I could hear my breath.

Light from distant streetlamps and high-rises cast a nebulous luminance over the deserted construction site. Rubble, cranes, debris, and equipment lay all around in the cavernous gloom. Piles of sand and ragged holes appeared here and there.

A few hard hats and worn-out black rubber boots sat near the silent machines and graying dumpsters. Cigarette butts littered the bulldozed earth.

Some distance away, a car roared by and interrupted the silence. Another car followed.

The air was heavily fetid with the workers' remaining sweat and the odors of the debris.

The midnight construction site felt like a lake, still and serene in the moonlight. I slipped out of my flip-flops and wiggled my toes in the cold dust, as if dipped in the soft lake water. A sense of calmness stole over me. I breathed deeply, drawing in the cool night air.

A gusty wind passed through. Safety vests dangling from a hook swung in the breeze.

The wind sliced right through my flesh to the bone, leaving an empty chill in its wake.

Skipping over dark holes, climbing into a crane cabin, descending a slope, and kicking at some empty cans, I wandered around the site.

Then, I found myself humming the song from a singing contest in Nan'an with the primary school's vice-headmaster playing *erhu*.

"*Lan lan de tian kong yin he li.*"

"Over the blue sky, there are silvery streams, the Milky Way."

The melancholy sound of *erhu* echoed in my head.

Worries dissolved into the tune.

The sorrows that I had been carrying mellowed, and their weight lifted. I breathed.

Tender was the wind's caress, a feathery touch upon the bare skin of my arm.

I walked and jogged away from the ravaged earth until my legs were sore and my adrenaline had subsided. At the exit of the catchment channel, I found a grass patch and sat on it, regaining my composure.

Tall bushes shielded me.

Drawing up my knees and wrapping my arms around them, I leaned back on the wall.

The moon was complete, clear, and close.

I gazed at the full moon and discovered that I could dream again. I dreamed that I returned to my unscarred, whole self.

The sound of my breath shrouded me and soothed me.

I rested my head on my kneecaps.

My eyelids grew heavier and heavier.

Just before I drifted off, a thing appeared.

A black, wolf-like dog stood in front of me. Its bones poked out of its flanks.

From ten feet away, the dog stared at me with its wide, gleaming eyes.

The eyes almost bulged out of its skull.

And when those eyes focused upon me, they turned livid.

"Do you know what I do to little girls?" challenged those dog eyes.

Slowly, I uncurled and shifted myself into a different position.

I placed my hands flat upon the ground, sitting erect, glaring back at it.

The dog tilted its head sideways, and I saw the moon in its left eye.

Neither of us flinched.

The moon's sharp light beamed through my brain, advising me to hold my ground.

I steadied my gaze.

Emboldened, I determined to protect myself and reclaim the dominion of my body.

So I raised my head, drew my shoulder blades together, and straightened my spine.

And then, I intensified my glowering at the black dog.

The sudden extension of my upper body and escalation of my spirit astounded it.

It cocked its head to the right and cowered slightly, still glaring at me.

But its muzzle lowered, and the light of its eyes dimmed.

It whimpered and slunk away.

A few times, it craned its neck to check on me.

I kept my posture and met the dog eye to eye.

When the dog's tail was entirely out of sight, I fell onto the grass.

Cool dew chilled me to the bones.

My sweat-drenched body shivered.

The Letter from Rainbow Village

The pressure helped to put things back together. I began to hear the drumbeat of my heart. *Ka-dom. Ka-dom. Ka-dom.* And then I heard a song that begins as follows.

> Don't ask me where I come from
> My hometown is far away
> Why do I wander
> Wander afar

It was *The Olive Tree* – a Taiwanese folk song sung by the singer Chyi Yu.

Chyi's voice is clean, tender, and yet powerful. Her angelic and natural delivery of the song transported me to another world. And the beauty of the song's melody touched the pristine place in my heart that no one could reach and corrupt.

The song's simple-worded, short, and elegant lyrics expressed a significant theme: longing and searching for freedom.

I listened to the song again and again. Gradually, there seemed to be a message embedded in the words waiting for me to decode. I put on my headphones and retreated, focusing on figuring out the message.

And then, one day, I heard:

Your spirit was intact. You were as free as ever to pursue your dreams.

And at the core of the song, I heard: Hope.

The lyrics and melody merged magnificently with Chyi's delivery of *The Olive Tree*. The song came alive. It glittered like the Milky Way bridge, inviting me to cross over, to lose myself in its astronomical swirl.

Another wondrous song of Chyi – *High Heels in September* – came out. It echoed *The Olive Tree* and continued to empower me. It begins like this:

Take off your lonely high heels
Ascend the small steps with your bare feet
And welcome to World Garden.

Again, hearing Chyi's pure, potent voice combined brilliantly with these transforming lyrics consoled me. It told me that there was somewhere else I could go, rest, and revive.

And then, I encountered Taiwanese writer Chiung Yao.
She also loved *Dream of the Red Chamber*.
Chiung Yao's debut novel – *Outside the Window* – spoke to me.
The book is about a seventeen-year-old, Yanrong Jiang, a high school girl who falls in love with her Chinese teacher, Kang Nan. He also falls head over heels for her. Yanrong comes from a reserved, well-educated family, and is well-read. Being sensitive, melancholic, and mischievous, Yanrong is full of ideas and imagination.
Kang is forty, a widower whose only daughter is also deceased. He becomes a lone eagle. But he is also a competent and devoted teacher. Students like him. Yanrong and Kang go through hell and do not get to live happily ever after.
Although I did not fall in love with my Chinese teacher, other things in the book touched me profoundly. For instance, Yanrong has a talent for writing, but her family frequently denigrates her. Also, I admired Yanrong's intrepid pursuit of love even after she fell into the trap of marrying someone else.
Outside the Window is an autobiographical novel broadly based on its writer and her early life in Taipei. It drew me close to her and her city.

Chiung Yao went on to write over fifty novels and became a massively popular romance novelist. Her books frequently feature women who go through years of intense psychological suffering for the sake of love. The male leads are often weaker than the female protagonists. Her plot lines tilt to the melodramatic side, and her dialogue can be long-winded.

The flaws in Chiung Yao's writing did not bother me too much. I enjoyed retreating to the worlds that she created. And I focused on the feminist aspects of her world.

Through her works, Chiung Yao permitted young women to break free from their families. She urged them to believe in themselves, knowing they could carve their own spaces in society and construct their lives as they saw fit.

Chiung Yao's encouraging messages and Chyi's inspiring songs generated a fierce force in me. It propelled me to open my eyes and see a better place beyond.

Through their art, I saw the doors of that place beyond were wide open like open arms. A warm sensation would travel through my body whenever I dreamt about that someplace else.

The sensation intensified. It solidified my belief day by day – if I could get to that place, I could gain freedom, flexibility, and fortitude.

I could rebuild my life.

Both Chyi and Chiung Yao came from Taiwan. So, Taiwan must be that place.

An island that was full of creativity and energy and inspirational artists – Taiwan – was that better place. I reconfirmed to myself.

Taiwan called me. I decided to accept the calling and act upon it.

Then, *Dream of the Red Chamber* returned to my mind.

I remembered that it was not until Baoyu left home for good that his father realized his value. And I recalled that the far side of the bed was where I belonged during those childhood storytelling times with my mother.

It was as if my fate was unfolding itself clearly and distinctly in front of me: I must leave home to find myself – the self that could sustain my life, making it worth living.

The summer holiday of 1990 came. Four more months, and I would be sixteen.

Starting in mid-June, I began my first job working at McDonald's. In the beginning, I could not handle customers' orders fast enough. It frustrated me because I feared losing my job to many other applicants who could replace me anytime.

But, *Outside the Window*'s Yanrong cheered me on by reminding me of the better world that awaited me. Such a prospect invigorated my mind and body, gradually making handling orders endurable and even pleasurable sometimes. So, I worked as many hours as I could get.

At the same time, I started gathering information about how to apply for a visa to Taiwan. Once I found out about the application methods and procedures through checking newspapers and conducting telephone inquiries, I applied for a Taiwanese visa in mid-August.

I made my Taiwanese visa application through Kong Wah Travel Agency (license no. 351059) under the Chinese Overseas Travel and Transport Service. The agency's address was 21/F, Euro-Trade Centre, 21-23 Des Voeux Road, Central, Hong Kong.

After I submitted my application to Kong Wah, they issued a receipt to me. The slip had my file number and an inquiry telephone number. This receipt is still with me today.

Besides paying bus fares, I had saved up all my salary from McDonald's since June. So, by the end of August, I had about $3,000 (about US$385). It might be enough to buy an air ticket to Taiwan and perhaps cover two weeks' hotel expenses.

I did not know what I would do after that. I would worry about it later. Yanrong would stand by me, and together, we would figure something out.

On the last Saturday morning of August, I received a notice from the Post Office to collect registered mail. It meant I could only get it on Monday – 1 September, my first day back at secondary school, Form 2 (Grade 8).

That last Saturday and Sunday of August were tremendous torture. I was worried sick about the outcome of my visa application.

The anxieties turned me into an ant running around a hot iron wok.

It was very doubtful that my visa application would be approved, as a fifteen-year-old with no prior record of traveling to Taiwan, who did not know anyone or have any supporters.

Indeed, no government in its right mind would grant a visa to a minor who applied alone. The iron wok got hotter, and my hope dimmer. Even Yanrong kept quiet.

By Sunday late afternoon, I was delirious.

While peeling a green apple with a sharp knife, I cut deeply into the flesh of my left hand's second finger. I kept staring at the blood gathered around the wounded fingertip, watching the assembled blood's size get bigger until it resembled a large teardrop.

Like an overflowing teardrop, it dripped from my palm, dropping to the ground.

And then, the scars near my wrists – the cigarette and iron burns – caught my eyes.

If I did not get the visa, I wondered what I would do to my body.

Maybe I would harm it further, more severely.

I needed more pain to numb my senses.

Then my school's Form 2 floor would be higher up, or maybe I could find the way up to the building's roof and silence all these horrible screams in my head with one jump.

The thoughts made my knees knock.

I tried desperately to think of something at home or school that interested me and that I could tether myself to – a reason for me to stay. Nothing came to mind.

*

Monday, 1 September 1990, finally arrived.

Strangely, I felt calmer than expected. Putting on my school dress, I had breakfast with my family except for my father, who usually had his earlier and left before others sat down. Then, I grabbed my schoolbag and pretended to go to school as usual.

But I hid in that corner beside the malodorous drainage ditch where I had my first cigarette. I waited there for all my family members to leave home. By eight, they were gone.

I sneaked back into our hut, changed into a white T-shirt and orange workers' jeans, and put on a pair of sports shoes. Also, I took a little time to write a note.

Dear Mother:

Writing this note to you feels like I was that eleven-year-old who corresponded and connected with you again. I was so glad I meant something to you and had your attention. Through your words, I imagined your smell, your heartbeat. My senses came alive when I read and reread your letters. I came alive.

Even though your frequent reply to my letters was primarily because of Younger Sister, I received them, which was good enough. But it all ended too soon. When Younger Sister and I rejoined you in Hong Kong, I seemed to lose my value.

It must be my fault, being unlovable, unworthy to be around you and everyone. So, I decided to leave. You and the rest of the family will live happier lives without me.

Have a fabulous life, Mother and all.

As for me, I will go somewhere else, where I can restart my life. I want to reinvent myself as someone worthy to be around, worthy of love.

Yours sincerely

Fongling

As I was staring at my note, I realized what hurt me the most was this sense of being "unworthy of love," which I felt whenever I was around my family.

Unworthy of love – this destructive sense seemed to legitimize the mental and sexual abuse that had happened to me so far.

It was as if being me deserved punishment.

Somehow, I knew this detrimental thought would follow me. It would continue to hurt, consume, and rot me.

But if I was lucky, I might survive.

That was the most I could hope for – for now.

I neatly folded the note, placing it in my mother's undergarments drawer.

Giving our hut a last look, I walked out, locked the rusty iron gate, and ran.

I did not look back even once.

After a while, I stopped to catch my breath.

The post office that I was going to was inside Rainbow Village.

I would get there in ten to fifteen minutes.

But my heart began to be laden with fears because my application might fail.

It ended up taking me double the time to get there.

Once I reached the post office and had the registered letter in my hands, I hurried out and turned right. Sitting on the ground, I leaned against the post office wall, curled up, and held the letter close to my chest.

I stared at the letter. My hands trembled.

Summoning up all the strength in me, I opened the letter.

The sight of a "Taipei Economic and Cultural Office (TECO) Hong Kong" bright red stamp leaped out at me. The gorgeous red logo glittered in the sunlight.

Yanrong's giggle made me realize I was holding the approved Taiwan visa in my hand.

I sprang to my feet and raised the visa, exclaiming:

"Hooray! Taiwan, here I come!"

To this day, I have no idea why the fifteen-year-old-me could obtain a Taiwanese visa alone. There must be a god who looks after broken people.

That same Monday, right after securing the visa, I headed straight to the Hong Kong Kai Tak International Airport.

All I brought was a small Nepalese blue-and-white striped cotton backpack.

Inside was my $3,000, my travel document (the Hong Kong Certificate of Identity issued a year after my arrival, which functioned like a passport), the Taiwanese visa, and one change of underwear.

In the summer, I had cut my hair, hoping to cut back my shame – the shame of a damaged girl. I looked like a boy with this head of short hair and sporty attire, and I felt different, better.

I arrived at the airport in Kowloon Bay, my first visit there. The excitement made my heart throb hard and fast. Eyes darting around the hall, I looked for the China Airlines counter. Many airlines, with hordes of advertisements, logos, and countless colorful counters, fought for my attention. It was nerve-wracking.

After a while, I singled out China Airlines and went to its ticketing section.

A graceful lady in uniform sat upright behind the counter. She formally greeted me. It was a moment that felt grown-up, significant, as if her greeting conferred on me the knowledge of that larger world out there, bringing it closer, making it palpably real.

Poised, I asked her:

"Can I buy a one-way ticket to Taipei, please?"

"A one-way ticket?"

"Yes, because I don't know when I will return yet."

"Oh, I see. What's your departure date, please?"

"Today. Now, actually. I wish to get on the next flight if possible, please."

"Really! Okay, there's one in about two hours. 14:25. Would it be too soon for you?"

"No, that's perfect. Thanks!"

And then, she learned that I was traveling alone. She regarded me for a second or two. Then she plunged into her work on the computer in front of her.

Suddenly, she raised her head and asked if I knew I needed a visa to go to Taiwan. I handed it to her, together with my passport.

The lady took both items, retrieved the visa from the passport, and held it close to her eyes. And then, her fingers brushed upon the words and the TECO stamp. She regarded me again with puzzlement.

"You are not yet sixteen, and you applied and obtained the Taiwanese visa yourself?"

I nodded.

Her eyes looked more bewildered.

She refolded the Taiwanese visa and inserted it between the last page and back cover of my passport, as I had done before.

She stood up and asked me to wait for her.

I nodded and followed her with my eyes.

She went to a man in a jacket sitting behind a corner table.

The two of them talked, and they looked my way in unison. They lowered their heads and discussed some more.

After what seemed like hours, the man gave the lady a nod while his eyes were fixed on me.

Uncertainty occupied his eyes.

I panicked.

The lady returned to the counter.

"I will issue the ticket for you right away."

I could not believe my ears.

When I heard the clicks of her keyboard, I sighed with relief.

And then I nearly jumped up with joy when she showed me the ticket.

Quickly, I paid the total amount, $1,480, as the lady told me, in cash.

She was processing it.

I could not stand still in front of her counter while waiting.

Gathering my willpower, I stood up straight and stared at the lady's lowered head.

The thought that if I showed my anxiety and lost focus by taking my eyes off her, she might change her mind and refuse to issue me the ticket, terrified me.

So, I kept standing erect and remained steadfast in my stare at the crown of her head.

About thirty minutes after I first approached the counter, she handed me the ticket – my first flight ticket.

A thrill rushed down my spine, enlivening my whole being.

The lady pointed to the departure gateway and instructed me to rush there.

I thanked her and hurried off. Before she could change her mind and confiscate my flight ticket, I ran toward the gateway without looking back.

The immigration checkpoint was behind me. No returning.

I headed to the departure hall and bounced to the gate.

A plane waited outside – my first flight.

I swiveled towards the plane like a plant toward sunlight.

Settling in a corner seat of the lounge, I faced the front of the plane. The plane's nose was so close, making me want to rub mine against it.

The cockpit windows were a pair of square eyes reflecting an iridescent blue, like a very calm sea surface. The sense of friendliness it conveyed invited me to look on. The simplicity and earthiness of the carrier's appearance exuded a sense of comfort.

A stream of staff went up and down the stairs that were temporarily attached to the plane. The afternoon sun sparkled gold across the aircraft and the team. An aura of calmness extended from the outside scene to somewhere inside me.

I sat back, smiled, and looked up.

The plane's erect tail captured all the sunlight.

The sharpness of it could easily slice through my flesh. I quivered.

Sliding further into the seat, I relied on its back and arm to shield me.

"China Airlines flight CI ... is boarding now. Please proceed to Gate ..."

The announcement jolted me out of my idle reverie.

People flocked to the gate. I rose and followed.

As I approached the aircraft, my steps became lighter and crisper.

A new future was awaiting.

I discovered and ventured onto this new path toward a different future alone.

Energy returned. And it felt like the tiger in me was reviving and regaining its power.

Inside the plane, I found my seat by the window.

Once I sat down, the outside view engrossed me.

Shafts of sunbeams spread across the airstrip, caressing the planes taking off and landing. The sunbeams looked as if they were giving me a farewell party and offering me their blessing.

Pressing my face against the window, I drank in the sunshine.

Yanrong smiled at me. I beamed with pleasure.

The air was getting warmer inside the plane as it filled up with passengers.

I relaxed and sank into my seat.

The plane started to taxi along the runway, and I began to doze off simultaneously.

In the next scene, I appeared in a beautiful white daisy dress and stood in a sunlit field, admiring the wildflowers. Gently, the flowers swayed in the breeze. I raised my head, feeling the falling petals caressing my face. The sun vanished. Darkness descended, devouring everything.

My heart pounded hard. My mind jerked back to reality.

I opened my eyes and looked around.

For a split second, I did not know where I was.

Guang! Guang! The engines cried.

The vibration of the engines caused the plane to shudder severely.

The take-off seemed almost vertical.

My hands gripped the arms of the seat while my eyes swept around the plane.

Restlessly, my body squirmed in the chair.

The plane finally stopped climbing.

I let go of the seat's arms, sat back, and breathed.

The harbor down below gave way imperceptibly to islands in the sea.

Then the islands disappeared too.

The ocean revealed her transparent happiness.

Such happiness found its way to me, giving me a warm glow.

I took a deep breath and rested my head on the back of the chair.

The afternoon sun remained strikingly luminous out there.

The man in the seat in front of me was reading a newspaper. He held it up against the window. A golden yellow spot seemed to appear in the middle of the sheet. The color deepened. It became an orange spot. In a split second, it was as if the orange circle had burst into flame. Then the flaming sheet, with the whirr of a liberated phoenix, resplendent in red, rushed out the window. It soared and joined the sun.

I closed my eyes and felt the warmth of the sunbeams starting to fill the room in my chest. It made me want to sing out loud:

> Don't ask me where I come from
> My hometown is far away
> Why do I wander
> Wander afar.

I laced my fingers, pushed my palms up and over my head, and at the same time, I put my legs together, lifted them, and straightened them out in front, giving my torso a good stretch.

Being a small person had its benefits. I smiled and settled back comfortably in the seat.

Awaiting my next destination, I replenished the shelves of my heart with hope.

Blithely, I looked out the window.

Snow-white clouds, myriad and feathery, were floating and forming a thick blanket.

Dream of the Red Chamber came to my mind.

In the fifth of the book's one hundred and twenty chapters, a scene describes a significant dream that Baoyu has. In it, he ascends to heaven and reads a manuscript of twelve *ci* lyric poems. The poems foretell the fates of the book's twelve main female characters. The last poem's final phrase is: "*luo le pian bai mang mang da di zhen gan jing.*" Or, "After all, only a shroud of whiteness remains in this world, which is so clean."

I felt clean and complete at that moment.

Part Four: Departure

Taiwan

1990 – 1992

The Capital City

The plane had been airborne from Hong Kong International Airport in Kowloon for some time and was heading steadily toward Taipei. I breathed easier.

An air hostess started to serve drinks. The man beside me helped her pass me a plastic cup of orange juice and got a beer for himself. When he sat back, I nodded to thank him.

He smiled and said:

"You're welcome. Are you going to study in Taiwan?"

His words were in Mandarin with a Taiwanese accent, similar to my southern Chinese one. Relaxed, I replied to him:

"Yes, but I want to find a job first."

My voice sounded almost alien to me, and it felt like I was underwater, where my words came from afar. It must be the effect of being in flight. If so, I might become different after this first flight and journey alone.

Perhaps my wish would come true – my old self will die, and from its fragments can come something new.

"You look too young for that. What kind of job are you looking for?"

Startled, I turned to look at the man and noticed his beer. It reminded me of my father, who, after a few drinks, would become loud and emotional. And then, my father always got upset with me for one thing or another, while my mother would disappear into the kitchen.

I recoiled into my seat and pursed my lips tight.

He cast a quizzical eye on me, making it impossible for me to avoid answering him.

I thought for a moment, drew a deep breath, and said:

"I want to find a job providing food and a place to live. So, I can save up the salary and attend school later."

"It seems like you've got a big plan!"

No, I did not. I tried to sound mature and credible, like I had it all figured out.

The truth was I did not have a plan.

But I had a dream. Something my parents would disapprove of had they known about it.

I sat straight, turned to the man, and replied with a calm smile.

A silence ensued.

He leaned backward but glanced at me keenly.

Angular-faced, of medium build, he looked to be thirty-something.

Many Taiwanese entrepreneurs set up factories in Shenzhen or Guangzhou following the economic reforms in China in the 80s. With this man's brown suit and polite but firm demeanor, he might be one of them or a manager who worked in one of those factories.

Suddenly, a grin lit up his face.

He sat up and said:

"You know, you can try the Taoyuan Industrial Area in the Taoyuan district, where our plane will land."

"Wait, you mean our plane will not land inside the Taipei city area?"

"Of course, it will not! It will land in Taoyuan district, the outskirts of Taipei."

"Oh, I see."

For the third time, he looked at me curiously.

I wondered why.

"Anyway, once you get off the plane, you need to find a bus that heads to the Taoyuan Industrial Area. Many electronic equipment manufacturing plants there always have openings. They like young apprentices."

He added enthusiastically:

"You can try your luck there!"

The excitement in the air made me speechless for a second.

"Whoa, that's so great to know. Thank you so much!"

"*Bukeqi.*" He smiled, genuinely happy for me, and said, "Don't be polite."

An announcement over the P.A. informed the passengers that the plane would be landing soon and ended our conversation.

I buckled up, sat back, and gazed out the window.

The ancient Chinese young woman warrior, Hua Mulan, came to mind out of the blue. At the end of *Mulan Ci*, *Ballad of Mulan*, she commits suicide to avoid becoming a servant to a foreign ruler.

When I decided to depart from my home in Hong Kong, I chose to stay alive. Mulan and I both took our lives into our own hands. It hit me: I could take up a new identity as the teenage Mulan who fought through wars and won. The Mulan-new-me could combat the difficulties and uncertainties of this unknown life ahead.

It would work. I would make it work.

Gray, dense clouds began galloping along the horizon.

A heaviness stole over me. I slid further into the seat and shut my eyes.

A splendid big blue sky greeted me when I walked out of the airport arrival hall.

Green mountains sat comfortably in the distance with patches of weightless white clouds adorning them. Afternoon sunlight embraced everything between the heavens and earth, and together, they exuded a sense of contentment.

The flat and vast landscape of Taoyuan and, by extension, Taiwan stunned me. It directly contrasted with the narrow, breathless, skyscraper-cluttered view outside Hong Kong airport that I had just left behind. It felt like a lifetime away already, though.

I threw my arms wide to receive the open skies, embracing the endless vistas of this vast, wondrous place.

Realizing I did not know how to proceed, I retreated to the arrival hall.

Two policemen stood in a corner area, observing the crowds. They stood about ten steps apart from each other, facing opposite directions. One looked out to the waiting crowds; another watched the passengers filing out from the last luggage checkpoint.

I went to the first one and found that the policeman appeared to be in his mid-twenties. Blue shirt neatly tucked into a pair of similar colored trousers, he wore a deep navy-blue vest on top, making him look intelligent and fit.

I got closer to the young policeman.

He had a boyishly handsome face.

It was Coach!

I froze solid on the spot.

Then, I began backpedaling.

But I kept telling myself to stop and look again.

It was not Coach.

The guy here was a different man.

I had left Hong Kong now.

Coach could not hurt me anymore.

I took a few deep breaths, making an effort to recompose myself.

A long moment afterward, I forced myself to walk toward the officer.

Two steps away from him, I stopped. My head had come up to the height of his chest. He was much taller than Coach.

Relieved, I stepped a bit closer and asked:

"Sir, can you please tell me where to take the bus to Taoyuan Industrial Park?"

He stared at me in silent concern.

"Why do you want to go to Taoyuan Industrial Park?"

"To find a job."

"What?"

His grave eyes inspected me all over.

"Officer, I want to find a job there."

I added urgently:

"You see, I need to work and save money to attend school afterward."

"Hang on, how old are you?"

"Fifteen. But I will be sixteen next month."

"What type of visa are you holding?"

"Tourist."

"But you can't work with a tourist visa!"

"Oh, is that the case?"

He quickly calmed himself and said:

"Yes, it is. It's against the law."

Looking at me with increasing concern, he asked:

"Is there anyone traveling with you?"

"No, sir."

"Do you know anyone here? I will be happy to make contact on your behalf."

"Thank you, but no, sir."

"You mean you travel alone, know no one here, and plan to work at fifteen with a tourist visa?"

Sensing that the answer "yes" could be problematic, my voice faltered into a tiny squeak when I squeezed the word out of my throat.

Never had I heard such a noisy quiet that followed.

His brow was frowning – two sharp parallel lines creasing on his head.

With trepidation, I looked away.

My heart became a pair of frightened wings trying to escape.

The policeman and I caught the attention of the other officer.

The second officer was shorter and slightly corpulent.

He strutted toward us. With slack and brownish skin, he might have been in his forties. His upright, broad shoulders carried a stronger sense of authority.

The younger officer explained the situation, taking only the slightest breath.

His senior colleague's eyes, sharp and shrewd, examined me the whole time.

His expression, neither cold nor frightening, remained neutral.

Maybe he encountered lost single teenage travelers like me all the time.

When the younger officer finished, I could only hear his short breath.

Imperceptibly, the sound faded, and the world ground to a halt.

I kept looking from one officer to the other, guessing what fate would befall me.

They might send me back.

I would need to face Hong Kong and my family.

Coach might come after me.

I gulped for air.

After his younger colleague's briefing, the older officer lowered his head.

He looked up, studying me.

Then he leaned his head toward the younger officer and gestured for him to do the same.

The senior officer did the talking in a low voice.

The younger officer nodded a few times in agreement.

Some long minutes later, the senior officer started moving away.

He paused and turned back to look at me after a few steps.

His glance brimmed with affection.

"Best wishes!" he mouthed with a wink and hurried off.

His warmth and geniality were so unexpected, they transfixed me.

My stomach quivered, and tiny flashes of happiness shot through my mind.

I bowed to him.

The younger officer took me to a deeper corner and said:

"Look, *Xiao mei-mei*," his addressing me as "Younger Sister" giving me hope.

"Let's act more discreetly and avoid further attention. Otherwise, I must follow the procedure and report you to the immigration officers. They will most likely deport you."

I stared at him with horror and kept quiet.

He continued:

"It's getting late now, so they may keep you for a night, liaise with the airline, and arrange for you to take the first flight back to Hong Kong tomorrow morning."

"Oh, please don't send me back. Please!"

Fear had its hand clasped to my throat, my dream smothered and choking.

"No, we won't."

Quickly, he went on:

"My colleague and I don't think you would want that either. We feel that you have tried very hard to get here. We believe you come with good intentions – something you want to achieve here. So, we have decided to do you a favor."

I gaped as I could not believe what I was hearing.

He continued:

"I'll bring you over to the counter of the National Taiwan University Overseas Chinese Student Association. You are lucky; school is starting. Senior students come here to assist the newly arrived students. They might be able to give you some help."

He looked at me earnestly and added:

"That's the best we can do for you."

"Thank you! Thank you very much!"

The police officer led me over to the counter of the student association in the airport arrival hall. He asked to speak to the person in charge.

A lanky, solemn-looking young man came forward and introduced himself.

The officer and the young man talked for some time. They then shook hands.

The officer turned to me and said:

"This person here is the vice-president of the student association. He is very kind and is willing to help you from here. National Taiwan University is considered the most prestigious university in Taiwan. You are in good hands."

As I parted my lips to thank the officer, no words came.

Trying again, I could only mouth the gratitude.

He gave me a nod and a smile of acknowledgment.

A tear was on my face. I could feel its damp, itchy path creeping down to my chin.

I wiped it away.

Watching me, he took his hand and laid it on my head.

The place where his hand was on me was melting with the warmth of that gentle touch.

"Good luck, *Xiao mei-mei*."

He paused for a moment and then turned to leave.

How long did I stare at his back?

His and his senior colleague's act of kindness heartened me.

The feeling of isolation had clung to me so fiercely and for so long that I forgot how hungry I was for human tenderness.

The two officers' willingness to believe in me unconditionally and their generous gestures rescued me as sure as if they had pulled me from drowning in the sea.

My head remained lowered when I heard a voice.

The sound reminded me of gently lapping waves.

"Hi, I'm Jizhou. Nice to meet you."

I looked up. The guy that the officer introduced spoke to me in Mandarin with an accent I could not locate.

"Oh, hi, I'm Fongling. Nice to meet you too."

We stood in front of the National Taiwan University Overseas Chinese Student Association counter at Taipei Taoyuan International Airport.

"Fongling, welcome to Taiwan."

"Thank you. It's so nice to be here."

"I'm from Malaysia and am the vice-president of the association. The policemen asked me to help you to get into a school here. But he also mentioned that you are holding a tourist visa. Is that correct?"

"Yes, that's correct."

"Unfortunately, it's almost 6pm now. The Education Department and the Foreign Student Office are both closed. I can't make inquiries on your behalf at the moment."

The tall Jizhou pushed his rimless glasses up and looked at me apologetically.

"I understand. That's too bad."

"Do you know any hostel?"

Seeing that I shook my head, he added:

"Or any area of the city you would like to stay in? I can find one and book it for you."

"Sorry, I have no idea at all."

My shoulders dropped as I felt the weight I brought on to him, this total stranger.

"It's okay," Jizhou said and smiled warmly.

He turned to two other students at the counter, and they exchanged a few words.

Turning back to me, he said:

"We are packing up and returning to our association's headquarters in Taipei. We have a few spare rooms in the headquarters. They are basic, but you are welcome to stay there tonight. We can think of something better tomorrow. Would you like that?"

My eyes burned, and my throat swelled up.

I nodded a few times in eager agreement.

After Jizhou and his classmates finished packing up, we got on a bus to the city.

Jizhou led me to a window seat, helped me to push the window open wider, and tied up the curtain before he settled into the seat next to me.

The other two students sat a few rows behind us.

There were no buildings, only fields and trees for a long while.

This landscape gave a completely different impression from Hong Kong, which was my only reference point for what a city looked like.

A sense of uneasiness took over. Nothing made sense.

The strangeness of the country view disorientated me, and it began to fill me with panic.

This bus was probably not going to Taipei city; it might be heading to the remote countryside instead. This journey would not end well.

I perched on the edge of the chair. Ready to run.

Streets with shops started to show up. The street lamps gave out a reluctant dull yellow glow. A scattering of low-rises came into view. They looked gray and timeworn and poorly built. More old houses appeared along with lanes of blackened walk-ups and countless shopfronts.

The city looked like it was thrown together in a hurry. But then, every few blocks, there would be a park with a generous supply of benches, shelters, and flowers. They told a story of a slower, simpler life.

I closed my eyes and inhaled deeply, letting in the earthy, refreshing air and releasing some anxiety.

The bus passed numerous street food vendors – their foods' fragrance, loud exchanges with the customers and the passers-by, and laughter replaced doubts with hopes.

Yet, the worries that these were all illusions and catastrophic events that would befall me were venomous snakes that spat and hissed underneath my skin.

Now shadows were looming everywhere.

Was that a tall man in a black cloak behind the bushes or a tumbling wall? Did you see that phantom? Could that be a tree? Why did that man look in my direction in such a malicious way? Did a black cat just run by, or did I blink my eye?

These peculiar thoughts had me bewildered.

I sat back and rested my head against the back of the chair.

Bright lights slanted through the window, inviting me to look again.

A night market emerged, heaving with people and stalls of CDs, toys, clothes, food, and drink. Vendors and customers talked and laughed a lot. Taiwan's air was in tune with its people; they both had an easy-going and earthy quality.

My clenched fists started loosening.

Westerners appeared among the locals; they interacted joyously using playful body language.

Suddenly, the melody of *The Olive Tree* drifted by. The song, coming from afar, felt like the sighing of the wind through the trees. It almost instantly created an atmosphere of peace and tranquility. I hummed along with the music and detected a sense of power returning to me.

I broke free from the gripping hand of fear and breathed.

It was the sweetest breath I had ever tasted.

A cluster of white butterflies with red and black heart-shaped dots decorating their wings but of different sizes hovered and lurched outside the window.

The blithe butterflies were celebrating their freedom in the warmth of my first night in Taipei.

NTU

After about two hours of the bus journey from Taoyuan Airport, Jizhou led me off.

The stop was right in front of the university's main gate. The other two students came and joined us.

I realized we were not heading toward the university campus as we walked. Instead, they turned to the main street facing the gate. I followed Jizhou, one step behind.

Soon, we entered a low-rise building by the roadside. On the second floor, there were two apartments. Jizhou told me that the association rented both flats. He opened the door to the left, held it, and let me and the other two in first.

The interior was in a simple, comfortable Japanese style. You had to take off your shoes and put them in the shoe cabinet at the entrance. Then you walked into a living room with tatami mats. The mats felt soft but firm to step on, a wondrous new experience for me. I took some small steps and almost smelled the rice straw on the mats.

The living room had a low square table, some cushions, two large bookshelves, and some cabinets. The table took the central position, with the pillows lying here and there casually. The full bookshelves stood tall in the corners, and the cabinets lined up against the wall on the opposite side. Three small rooms with futon mattresses and quilts neatly folded on the floor connected to the living area.

In small groups, students gathered in the living area or those rooms and carried out their conversations quietly.

It felt right to be there.

After settling in, Jizhou went out. He returned with two bowls of Taiwan braised beef noodles and offered me one for dinner. I realized how hungry I was when I finished it in less than ten minutes, even with the hot soup.

Some more students came in. Jizhou told me the association had a meeting scheduled for that night and gave me a briefing.

Earlier that year (1990), Taiwan had had a significant social event – the "Wild Lily Student Movement." It was the first large-scale social movement started by Jizhou's fellow local students of National Taiwan University.

Jizhou told me that on 16 March, about seven of the NTU students staged a sit-in at Chiang Kai-Shek Memorial Hall, like the square in Beijing, albeit much smaller. The event occurred after the National Assembly's aged members abused their power and extended the terms of the "people's representatives."

The unjust and outdated gerontocracy triggered this monumental movement.

Jizhou (who, of course, was Malaysian) learned that the local students revolted against the ancient and authoritarian political system that had oppressed them all their lives. When other students across the island received the news about the demonstration that night, they rushed in to show solidarity.

The number of participants peaked at four or five thousand students, with many first-time protesters. They felt the time had come for them to stand up and demand immediate constitutional reform.

However, the students admitted that they only had an abstract idea about democracy. They only knew it was good and that they wanted it. The local young people grew up in an education system that force-fed them and kept brainwashing them into preparing for exams and being obedient. They encountered numerous political taboos that restricted them from getting involved in politics.

In the 1980s, the government incarcerated dissidents regularly, and alternative voices were nonexistent. The March movement marked the beginning of people speaking out publicly and criticizing the government. It was new, noble, and unstoppable.

The NTU students organized the protests in peaceful ways. From dawn till dusk, they kept everything under control even when the number of attendees became almost overwhelming.

Finally, their actions and voices had caught the attention of President Lee Teng-Hui, who agreed to meet and implement some reforms.

The main agenda of the meeting was to compare and contrast the Wild Lily movement with the incident that had occurred in Beijing a year earlier.

When Jizhou invited me to the meeting, I felt grown-up and honored.

The apartment's door opened, and a tall, broad-shouldered young man walked in. Jizhou stepped forward to chat with him. Turning their heads toward me, Jizhou made an introduction. I learned that the guy was Yusheng, the president of the overseas student association.

Yusheng sat at the head of the square table with Jizhou and me by his side. The students spread out and over the living room.

Once the meeting began, a student immediately asked for my opinion because I had just come from Hong Kong, which, to her and others, was much closer to Beijing.

The students' eyes were on me, thrilling and frightening. To be taken seriously felt incredible, but I did not have any original comments about the protests.

Maybe it was because the patriotism that I had inherited from my mother prevented me from registering and recalling the incident.

I apologized to the students profoundly, moved back toward the wall, and made myself as small as possible. I did not want to catch further attention and cause disappointment.

But I stayed focused and listened to them attentively. It was time to view my country from an alternative angle and learn narratives other than my mother's.

Jizhou offered his interpretation of the current political climate and its effect on the students' situation and stated his solidarity suggestions.

Another student raised his concerns. He disagreed with some of the activities Jizhou proposed. Yet another jumped in and gave her opinions.

The discussion, full of passion and ambition, moved at top speed.

My eyes dashed from one student to another, observing their speaking styles.

The participants excelled at expressing themselves; their free spirits, knowledge of themselves, and what they believed impressed me immensely.

After the meeting, Jizhou asked me to call home. It came as a shock.

I told him that it was unnecessary. But he insisted.

From the convenience store, he had earlier purchased an international calling card. He scratched a silvery strip off the card, and a password appeared. He read the instructions on the back of the card, asked me to give him the number, and began to dial.

There was no way I would speak to my family and let them know where I was.

Not now. Probably never.

Once the phone started ringing, Jizhou handed the handset over to me.

"Hello."

Luckily, the neighbor girl and not one of her parents picked up the phone.

"Haiyan, how are you? It's Fongling here."

"Fongling, where are you? Your family is looking for you."

"It's okay. I'm okay. Please tell my parents not to worry."

"Oh, okay. But where are you?"

"Sorry I can't tell you now. Please just tell them I'm safe."

"Okay, I will."

"Thanks, Haiyan. Bye."

"But… oh, bye."

I put down the phone and told Jizhou that everything was fine.

As the telephone conversation was in Cantonese, Jizhou had no idea what I was saying.

Years later, I learned that my call had caused Haiyan tremendous trouble.

A few days after my call, my school class teacher urged my parents to report my disappearance to the police. At first, my parents saw it as a great shame for the family and did not want to disclose it, especially to the authorities. They did not wish to have anything to do with the police, fearing trouble. And they did not want to lose face by admitting such a shameful event to relatives and outsiders.

But my class teacher spoke to my parents time and again. He asked them to let go of their egos and realize that finding me and ensuring I was safe should be the priority. Reluctantly, my parents acquiesced.

When the police took on the case and learned that I had called Haiyan, they kept questioning her to see if she had known about my plan to run away. Haiyan told them repeatedly that she did not, which was true. I had kept it all to myself.

But because of that call, the police continued to interrogate Haiyan. And they asked her from time to time if I called her again. No, she told them, which was also correct.

The police assumed she was my best friend. But the truth was I did not have any friends in Hong Kong back then.

The next day, Jizhou needed to resume duty at the airport. Before he left the apartment, he told me that Yusheng, the president, would take care of me that day.

Yusheng arrived and asked me to take my luggage. He had found a new place for me to stay temporarily. I picked up my small blue-and-white cotton backpack and was ready to go with him.

Yusheng stood, stared at me, and asked:

"That's all you are traveling with?"

I nodded. My newly cut, short hair moved forward.

"Yes. I don't want to carry too many things from my old life here."

"But you are only fifteen! Why do you call it an old life?"

"It's a long story. I will tell you another day."

But I never told him.

Not even Jizhou knew the whole story of why I left home and went to Taiwan alone.

Yusheng opened the door, and out we went.

We crossed the street and walked toward National Taiwan University's main gate.

An inscription of the six Chinese characters *Guo Li Tai Wan Da Xue* or "National Taiwan University" (NTU) in calligraphy appeared atop the gate.

The style of the calligraphy gave out an unconventional impression. It did not inherit any particular genre that I could recognize. Instead, it looked more like a combination of several types. With its cursive and semi-cursive style, it felt unique and original.

The calligraphy's aesthetic qualities were inspirational and admirable – features of NTU which, as I later learned, is the oldest and most outstanding Taiwanese university.

I stepped through the gate and entered NTU. Yusheng walked close by me.

It was 2 September 1990. Instead of attending Form 2 in Hong Kong, I succeeded in arriving in Taipei alone and entering the campus of a prestigious Taiwanese university.

I clenched my fists in determination to grasp this opportunity – the turn of my fate.

How I wished to bottle this moment: the moment that I felt everything was possible.

Like the four-year-old me under the fascinating full moon, I kept dreaming.

The university's main avenue opened wide in front of me.

Tall coconut palms lined both sides of this central road. The long, green leaves swayed gently in the wind.

A sign showed that the road was called *Ye Lin Da Dao*, or Royal Palm Boulevard.

This broad green avenue set the whole campus's tone: graceful and open.

It told the story that this university could embrace all kinds of people, giving them space.

To learn. To grow. To excel.

Two walking paths ran parallel to both sides of Royal Palm Boulevard.

A riot of flowers adorned these two paths.

As we walked, Yusheng, an agriculture major who loved plants, told me that the flowers included blue sky flowers and Japanese beautyberries. He pointed to some little leaves and bell-like purple flowers and told me their name was millettia.

Some students occasionally stopped to marvel at the flowers.

Others walked on, rushing to their classes, hurrying to pursue their dreams.

I admired these university students. They belonged to this beautiful, intellectual world.

Yusheng did not lead me down the university's main avenue. Instead, he took a right turn, and we ventured onto a path for a few minutes. Then, a building appeared in front of us.

Yusheng told me that that was House One, one of the female dormitories of NTU.

As we approached the gate, a young lady came and greeted us.

Yusheng made the introduction. The lady was his girlfriend, Cheer.

Cheer was an ethereal beauty with an aura of elegance surrounding her slim body.

She had a head of long, soft, curly hair that swayed gorgeously when she walked.

I was mesmerized by Cheer's charm as she reminded me of my elder sister, whom I adored but who never warmed to me.

Lost in my thoughts, I forgot to say goodbye to Yusheng before he left.

Cheer took me into her room in House One.

She let me stay in an upper bunk bed that belonged to a Japanese student named Hiroko. Hiroko lived with her boyfriend in a flat off-campus most of the time.

Two other roommates stayed there with Cheer as well, and they were Shinyi from Malaysia and Meiching from Tainan in southern Taiwan.

Once Cheer, Shinyi, and Meiching knew I did not have any other clothes, they dug out their small-sized garments and gave them to me.

The other neighboring students learned about me and my situation, and they also brought and offered me theirs. I ended up having a big pile of clothes at my disposal.

The best thing about having their clothes was that I could wear them and pretend that I was one of them, a real student there.

But every night, I had to take them off, return to my runaway self, and resume the identity of the person who did not know what would happen to her the next day.

I could be caught and sent back to Hong Kong at any moment.

Despite everything, I tried my best to get on with my life on campus.

I treasured every minute, every day, while it lasted.

As a result, I lived in the present and completely immersed myself in this new "university life."

*

Cheer, Shinyi, and Meiching provided food for me too.

One would take me to the student canteen on the dormitory's lower ground floor daily. Depending on their time and the number of meal tickets available, I would have breakfast, lunch, or dinner – one meal a day.

Then, Meiching came up with an idea to help me make some pocket money. She suggested that I copy the theses of the students by hand. Many students supported Meiching's idea. They gave me their drafts to copy and gladly offered me NT$500 (about US$17 at the time) for the five thousand words I copied.

I did this copying job with all my heart.

In the process, I learned about thesis writing – how the piece was structured and how the ideas were presented, argued, and validated.

Also, I listened to their classes and drank in the knowledge like a parched desert traveler.

Furthermore, whenever I encountered new vocabulary, I would try and memorize it.

This job was a great gift to me. I could not believe my fortune: living in an eminent environment surrounded by kind and stellar university students.

Counting my blessings, I lived every day, learning and evolving.

Spring swung by, and azaleas did not use words to announce their arrival to the world; they simply bloomed.

In March, azaleas flowered elegantly across the university campus. The flower blossom transformed the campus into an endearing and unforgettable scene for everyone to enjoy.

Consequently, the campus was hailed as the "City of Azaleas" for its spectacular blossoming. The university also boasted of having a great diversity of azaleas. It was true.

NTU   157

Looking around, you would find myriad flower hues displaying their distinctive beauties – so blithe and carefree.

The vibrant azaleas absorbed me. I often strolled along Royal Palm Boulevard at the heart of the campus and let the power of the blooming azaleas energize me.

Sometimes, I got very jealous of the azaleas, for they had a strong sense of belonging.

The campus welcomed and treasured the flowers; the professors, students, and visitors admired them. On the contrary, I often doubted myself and my right to be there.

Those thoughts were heavy. They caused me to lower my head when they invaded me.

But with my bent head, I noticed the petals on the ground. Piece by piece, I gathered them up. After I got a big bunch of them, I buried them and made a flower cemetery for them as Daiyu did in *Dream of the Red Chamber*.

And then I remembered that I had burned and buried my diary. It was one of the reasons I ran away from home. The recollection pained me.

I quickly shifted my attention to happier scenes right before me.

The university held the Azalea Festival each year, and it became a well-known tradition on the entire island and beyond. The festival expanded – incorporating diverse activities such as expositions, art exhibitions, and ecological tours. These were public events. Groups upon groups of high school students came and participated. They were very keen to glimpse this top university in Taiwan that they aspired to attend.

Amid the outsiders, I relaxed somewhat. When I regarded the azaleas again, they symbolized youth, intellectualism, possibility, and happiness.

Beneath the flowers, international artists performed; painters set up their panels to draw or sketch on their pads; photographers busied themselves trying to capture the blossoms' glory from various angles; lovers took pictures of each other or asked someone else to shoot them. Cheers and claps and laughter broke out from time to time.

The campus was full of festive, liberal, communal, and all-encompassing spirits.

My heart brimmed with hope.

Xiao Mei Wanted

I started a part-time job in a teashop outside the campus.
It was about two months into my stay at the dormitory.

Amy, an alumna of the university, owned the teashop. She learned about my situation from a current student and decided to help me.

Amy let me work three times a week over lunch hours. That way, I earned a few extra dollars and, more importantly, had another meal guaranteed.

One day, after the lunch rush hour, I cleaned all the dishes, restaurant, and kitchen areas with another student helper. When it was about 4pm, I left Amy's teashop.

For some reason, I did not feel like going back to the dormitory. So, I began wandering around the narrow alleys nearby and found Japanese, western, and local restaurants all over the passages, and they were close to each other.

After a while, I got lost in the labyrinth of the alleys. Since I had time, and the daylight still shone, I did not worry but continued to stroll.

The buildings were low rises – dark roofs, gray walls – pretty ugly. But the restaurants were decorated with gardens and natural themes, at least in the front yards where I could see.

When I turned a corner, a small wooden door appeared.

It seemed to present itself to me solemnly.

A tiny red notice stood out in the upper middle of the wooden gate.

It said: "*Xiao Mei* Wanted."

In this context, *Xiao Mei*, Little Sister, could mean waitress or helper.

I could do with another part-time job.

So, I gave the door a light push. It opened, and I stepped in.

The area in front of me was a low porch for the guests to take off their shoes. Three steps led to an upper level. The floor was dark brown wood.

"Is someone here?" I called out.

Silence.

"Yes, coming…," a husky female voice answered me.

Then, a woman in her fifties emerged from the gloom.

She was slender and wore a kimono. Her eyes were piercingly feral, her face thick-powdered and mask-like, her lips scarlet and shiny, resembling a bright red traffic light.

Standing tall and near the upper level's edge, she loomed.

The dark background. The low ceiling. The appearance of such an eccentric old lady.

Instinctively, I turned toward the door, trying to get out.

"Wait!"

She rushed down the three steps and headed to me.

Before she arrived in front of me, her perfume assailed my nostrils. It was heady and rosy and so overpowering that for a second, I felt disoriented – my head swimming.

"What's your name?"

"Oh, er… my name is Fongling."

"Fongling, what a lovely name. It's as lovely as you."

I blushed and lowered my head.

Her hand touched the tip of my chin and lifted my face a little.

"What an adorable face, indeed."

She smiled and continued.

"But young lady, you are way too skinny. I'm going to have dinner. Come, join me."

Like a balloon, my head expanded with the air of her attention and approval. It was not my first time receiving praise for my looks, as I was once called a "Form 1 Fairy". But this was different. She was a senior who had seen many people; what she said had much more weight.

The woman ceased to be scary. And her dinner invitation sounded so casual and ordinary, like she had been waiting for me.

Feeling so special, I followed her.

We walked through a living room.

It was quite a large area with a stage and a screen at the back, a small TV set in front, and a microphone next to it. Many small rooms surrounded the living room as rows of doors covered the walls along the sides.

My eyes kept dashing about, trying to figure out the functions of those rooms.

We passed through a dimly lit corridor. But I could see some tiny lightbulbs inside the walls and realized there were built-in cabinets. Through the lightbulbs inside the cabinets with glass doors, bottles and bottles of wine and whiskey appeared, with some lying in racks while others stood tightly next to each other on the bottom shelf.

We turned a corner, she pushed open a door, and we stepped into a kitchen.

A square table sat next to a wall with three chairs around it. About a step away, there was a fridge and a sink. The two of us took up the remaining space.

The woman asked me to take a seat.

She went to the refrigerator and took out some food.

"Do you like sushi?"

"Yes."

I had no idea what it was.

"Good, let's eat."

The look of the unfamiliar food reminded me that I was with a stranger in a strange place.

Then, it evoked a question in my head about my reason for being there.

I looked at the woman and said:

"Madam, you may know I am here to apply for the *Xiao Mei* post."

Seeing that I had her attention, I went on.

"May I apply, please?"

"Yes. And you are hired."

I tried to suppress my smile – how special I must be.

"Thank you, Madam. I won't disappoint you."

It did not occur to me to ask about the salary. So far, all my encounters in Taiwan had treated me better than I ever expected. I believed this woman would reward me reasonably, too.

She turned to me, nodded, and said:

"Call me *Ayi*."

She asked me to call her "auntie". Wonderful.

"Ah… *Ayi*, sorry, I can only work part-time. Is this okay with you?"

"Yes, it's perfect."

She handed me a cup of water, a pair of chopsticks, and a plate with what must be sushi.

I waited for her to sit down and eat so I could copy her method.

We ate in silence.

Then, a commotion broke out. The noise of some girls talking and laughing filled the corridor.

I looked at *Ayi*. She urged me to eat up.

Someone pushed the door open.

A woman in her early twenties appeared.

Upon seeing me, she said:

"New blood? And so young and pretty? Lucky you, Mamasan!"

Behind her, a group of five or six similar-aged women giggled.

I flushed – happy to be praised again.

The young woman closed the door and walked away with the others.

Her words lingered. Their titters and footsteps rang loud.

Amazed, I turned to *Ayi* and asked:

"Why did she say you are lucky?"

"Because of you! Your arrival is a gift from the goddess to me."

Now I felt super special.

So I ate as fast as possible.

The cold rice and raw fish seemed only to grow larger in my mouth. Swallowing hard, I drank the cup of water in one gulp, washing down the food.

Ayi took me to the room adjacent to the kitchen.

The young women's chatter sounded close. They must be getting changed as one asked another to help zip up; yet another complained that her dress had become too tight. Then, further off, probably from the restaurant area, came some men's voices and music.

Ayi opened a cupboard and took out a red silk *qipao* – a body-hugging, one-piece traditional Chinese dress.

She admired the dress for a second and sighed.

Then she turned to me and said:

"I used to wear this when I was young and fresh, just like you."

She smiled, maybe at herself, sadly.

Then she shook her head and chirped:

"You can wear it tonight."

The *qipao* shimmered and blinded my eyes.

I had never worn an expensive skirt, let alone a deluxe dinner dress.

It was the kind of outfit I imagined a Chinese bride would wear on her wedding night.

"But why... I am only a waitress, right?"

"Yes, but you are my pride and joy!"

Reinforcing her words, she beamed and continued:

"Our clients are important people. I want to dress you and present you to them properly. They will think as highly of you as I do."

I must have looked worried as she added quickly:

"Trust me. The VIPs will adore you if you wear this dress."

I felt wings growing out of my shoulders, as if I was going to fly.

"Come, let me help you to change into this."

She pulled the *qipao* over me.

The dress was as snug a fit for my body as a new skin.

I looked into the mirror and dreamt of myself as a lost and found Chinese princess.

But then, *Ayi* stared at my chest for too long.

My cheeks began burning as I hated myself for disappointing her.

She must have sensed my guilty and terrible feelings because she put her hand tenderly on my shoulder and gave me a little squeeze.

I stood straight and found it hard to breathe.

She returned to her wardrobe, retrieved two pads, and walked back.

Standing before me, she asked me to unbutton, loosen the dress's upper part, and unclasp my bra.

I was too embarrassed to do so and did not move.

She smiled and went ahead to unbutton my dress.

She unclasped the bra and let it hang loose.

"Bend your upper body slightly forward, please," *Ayi* instructed.

I quickly did so.

She inserted a pad into each side of my bra underneath my breasts.

Her hands held the pads and pushed up my breasts.

She asked me to close my bra when she removed her hands.

Once she made sure the pads were in place, she buttoned up my dress.

She stepped back and inspected me.

"Stay still."

I did so.

She nodded as if to say good.

Then she focused on my face.

Quickly, she took out something from her bag and started to powder my face.

She touched a small case with a pink color in the middle and circled my cheeks for a few rounds using a brush. She licked up some glossy red lipstick with a silvery, small, pointy brush and applied it to my lips.

My body stayed rigid the entire time.

Looking pleased, she put away the things and said:

"That's my girl. Come with me now."

I passed a mirror on the way out and could not recognize the person reflected there: with my quick makeover, a double of *Ayi*, albeit her younger self, had emerged.

The reflection got me in a flap, and it gave me a sense of tremulous excitement at the same time.

We came to the living room.

It was full of men who wore suits and ties, though many had loosened them.

A man's coarse singing voice invaded the air. The song's lyrics were incomprehensible. After a while, I realized it was a Japanese *enka* [ballad]. The man sang on the stage facing the TV screen. He immersed himself in the song, sounding incredibly sad and nostalgic for lost love.

The young women I met previously wore lacy, princess-like dresses.

They sat in between the men at different tables.

Some men were playing dice, drinking, or smoking.

The women squeezed themselves among the men.

Some women clapped their hands; some chatted with the men.

They laughed, drank, and pressed their bodies against each other as if for warmth.

The reek of tobacco hung in a thick cloud. It made my throat dry and constricted.

Ayi squeezed my hand. We walked on and reached a door.

She knocked.

We entered.

It was a relatively large but irregular-shaped room, faintly lit.

In a low-cut evening gown, a young woman sang on a triangular corner stage.

A romantic song with soft music filled the room. Men and women were in each other's arms, dancing.

Ayi closed the door behind me.

My muscles tensed up.

A harsh rose scent impregnated the air and took up too much space in my lungs.

I felt light-headed and nauseous.

The man sitting in the middle of a sofa was smiling at me.

My body quivered.

The ladies around him giggled but stopped once he gave them a glimpse.

In his forties, the man had a square, imposing brow and neat hairstyle.

A few lines appeared upon his forehead, but they dissipated as if tricks of the light.

His eyebrows were impossibly straight, and his eyes took on a rich, engrossing darkness.

Ayi led me toward the man.

He stood up.

The two women beside him got up at once too.

And then, they seemed to glide out and exit in silence.

Ayi gave the man my hand, and he took it immediately. His warm hand made me realize how cold mine had been.

"Be a good girl and listen to him," *Ayi* murmured.

I wanted to cry:

"No, no, no, please don't leave me!"

But no voice would come out.

The man sat me down.

Like a small wooden doll, I did.

He moved closer to me; his thigh brushed mine.

I recoiled.

His cologne enveloped me.

The singer switched to a disco song.

Others carried on dancing.

The noises were drowning me.

Frantically, my eyes searched for help.

Ayi got close to the door.

I fixed my eyes on her back.

Like a miracle, she turned around.

I caught her eyes – a sense of pity was there.

She went out and shut the door behind herself quickly.

I sat upright, realizing I could count on no one but myself.

"It's never easy the first night," the man whispered.

I nearly jumped out of my seat and knocked over the glass in front of him.

"Don't worry. I will take good care of you."

His voice was softly mellifluous.

His deep, dark eyes locked on to mine. Those eyes of his were trying to pull my whole body toward him.

Then his hand came atop my thigh.

My legs shuddered.

I felt sick.

Quickly, I searched for the toilet sign.

"It's outside the door and down the corridor. You will find it on your left."

Then his mouth came close to my ear and breathed:

"Come back soon. I'm right here waiting for you."

He put his right hand on my lower back to stress his words.

The heat of his palm sent ripples of fear through my body.

I leaped up and hastened to the door.

Once I was out of the room, I did not go down the corridor toward the toilet.

Instead, I bolted toward the living room.

Bracing myself, I pushed through the throng and hurried toward the front door.

Shouts and laughter caught up to me.

Someone tried to grab me. I pushed on.

"Stop her!" *Ayi* yelled.

I kept running.

Then, I reached the steps connecting the upper ground to the lower floor.

The door was right in front of me.

My back foot caught my front foot. I fell forward.

My hand reached out and got hold of the door handle.

I took a deep breath, thrust the door open, and ran.

It was after midnight when I returned to the dormitory using an inconspicuous side door. I waited a long time in a dark corner near it, ensuring nobody used it before I went in.

I could not let anyone see me wearing a *qipao*.

Creeping up the stairs, I tried not to wake anyone.

Quietly, I sneaked into the room.

It was dark, but I remembered where I put my pajamas.

I changed into them, rolled the *qipao* into a ball, brought it up to my bunk, and put it next to the pillow, close to the wall.

After a week, I summoned all my strength one afternoon and decided to return the *qipao* to its owner. It took me close to an hour to find the place. When I saw that unassuming wooden door, my heart thumped violently.

I put the dress beneath the postal box, gave the door a few loud knocks, and ran. Later, when I changed to a fast walk, it struck me. There was no sign saying "Xiao Mei Wanted" any more.

Pai Hsienyung

Like the sexual assault I experienced, I kept this new terrifying incident to myself.

Over time, I excelled at keeping secrets, at least during the day. The untold horrors gave me sleepless nights, replaying loudly and clearly in my head.

The internal screams were severe self-reprimands, as I criticized myself for being vain and superficial. It all felt like my fault. I must have brought these horrible events upon myself.

And I realized then that if, instead of the two kindhearted police officers, I had met the like of *Ayi* at the airport and went with her, I could have ended up in a brothel and become a prostitute.

The thought terrorized me.

I sat up in bed at night because when I lay down, I found breathing very hard.

After some time, I sought consolation in books again. The library of the university became my refuge.

Through reading, I reembarked on my journey of learning.

Familiarizing myself with Taiwan seemed urgent. So I started reading about it.

Among the Chinese, we call Taiwan *Bao Dao*, the Treasure Island, because the place has rich soil that produces abundant, superb quality agricultural products. Also, its inhabitants are hard workers.

Regarding Taiwan's shape, some people say it looks like a whale or dolphin, and many more reckon it looks closer to a sweet potato. But to me, it resembles a small boat floating on the edges of the Pacific Ocean – Japan to its north and the Philippines to its south.

Over time, Taiwan's population has included indigenous tribes, Dutch, Spanish, Japanese, Han Chinese, and, more recently, Americans. Together, they have created a varied culture and developed different local customs and traditions along the way.

And then, I encountered Pai Hsienyung through those readings in the university's library.

Pai is a renowned and broadly recognized contemporary Chinese writer.

It was thrilling to learn that he came to Taiwan when he was fifteen, the same age as me.

Pai was born in Guangxi, China, in July of 1937 as the Second Sino-Japanese War was breaking out. In 1952, the fifteen-year-old him went to Taiwan to join his father, a high-ranking Nationalist general.

Pai studied in the Department of Foreign Languages at National Taiwan University – the same university I stayed in. During his university years, Pai founded *Modern Literature* magazine and published stories such as *The Elder Mrs. King*, *The Moon Dream*, and *Yuqing Sao*.

In 1963, Pai left for the United States and joined the Writers' Workshop at the University of Iowa. Two years later, he completed his Master of Fine Arts degree. In an interview, he said those two years of study greatly influenced his writing skills and artistic style in fiction.

Pai loves *Dream of the Red Chamber* and believes it is one of the world's best novels. He taught the book at the University of California, Santa Barbara, for over twenty years.

Among Pai's many excellent books, such as *Taipei People*, *Crystal Boys*, *Jade Love*, and *The New Yorker*, I felt the closest to the first. *Taipei People* consists of fourteen stories, and they are about the mainland Chinese, or Mainlanders, who fled to Taiwan in the 1950s and their lives and struggles then.

Pai lived in Hong Kong for only three years, but his Cantonese is better than his Taiwanese Hokkien. The difference might be due to his young age, his chance for daily immersion in the language, and the communication he could have with the local people.

While he lived in Taipei, because of his father's power struggle and personal grudges with Chiang Kai-Shek, the Nationalist party leader, Pai's family residence was constantly under surveillance by secret agents, despite being away from the isolated "veterans' villages" where most of the Kuomintang soldiers' families lived. As a result, his contact with outside society was limited.

The isolation could be why his Hokkien is not as fluent as his Cantonese and why the characters in his stories are mostly not based on ordinary Taiwanese. Outsiders are particularly prominent in *Taipei People*.

Following the War of Resistance against Japan, the Chinese Civil War, and the founding of the People's Republic of China in 1949, many Mainlanders fled to Taiwan, either directly or via Hong Kong. The stories in *Taipei People* reflect these Mainlanders' experiences.

Two stories inside this collection had the most significant impact on me.

One was *A Sea of Blood-red Azaleas*. It is about a servant called Wang Hsiung who epitomizes the torment of exile. I learned from the story that the Azalea symbolizes homesickness and exile in Chinese culture. Also, the symbolism "fish out of water" pervades the narrative. It reminded me of how I felt when I went from mainland China to Hong Kong when I was twelve. Identifying with Wang gave me the warmth and energy to go on as a wayfarer.

Another story that had a strong appeal to me was *Autumn Reveries*. Autumn suggests aging, and the narrative depicts both the power and fragility of beauty. I could not understand these themes well, but I liked the recurrent chrysanthemum in this tale.

My mother told me that the fragrance of chrysanthemum surrounded her on the morning of my birth as the flowers blossomed gloriously outside her bedroom window.

Later, I also learned that in Chinese culture, which is reflected in this story, the chrysanthemum specifically represents the transience of life. This particular flower has a brilliant yet brief blooming before its inevitable decline.

I did not mind having a short life so long as I could find my brilliance and live it out.

East Met West

The College of Liberal Arts was a place I frequented as I sat in the literature lectures.

One day, a poster introducing a public talk caught my attention as I passed the lecture hall door. The event was taking place on that day and at that time.

Discreetly, I gave a light push on the door and peeked in. The talk had just begun. I crept in and sat in the back row. The seats came in descending rows, looking down toward the stage.

The speaker wrote something on the green board, turned around, and picked up some notes. He appeared artistic, amiable, and wise, in his late forties – a man of great charm.

He had a head of wavy hair, as wavy as the sea waves, an angular face, and a pair of dark, decisive eyes. His attire was sharp and simple – a black T-shirt, a white shirt on top paired with black trousers. He exuded elegance.

Glancing steadily across the lecture hall, he smiled and put everyone at ease.

Sunbeams ran through the windows, dancing. The hall was flooded in warm late-morning sunlight together with the attendees who waited for a literary feast to begin.

A deep, sonorous voice emerged and gripped me immediately.

It was from the speaker who started reciting a poem.

The words of the poem rolled from his tongue like pearls:

It is hard for us to meet and too soon to part
Eastern winds weaken; flowers wither

The silkworm stops weaving when it's dead
The candle stops weeping when it burns out
At dawn, she fears finding gray hair in the mirror.
At night, she senses the moonlight's chillness and chants the
evening song towards Penglai (the Enchanted Mountain) which
is not far off.
I hope the bluebird will go there and bring me that person's
news.
(My translation)

I recognized it as an untitled poem by Li Shangyin, written for an
unnamed person.

The speaker cast his eyes far off when he finished reciting the poem.
It looked as if he wished the bluebird would visit the one he missed and
bring him some news.

Suddenly, he swept his eyes across the lecture hall, and I lowered my
head instantly.

It was legitimate for me to sit in the lecture, especially this public one.
But somehow, I found it difficult to allow myself to be there, be amidst
the elite academics and students, and relish such a delicious lecture.

"Do you know who can understand Li Shangyin the best?"

The speaker looked to the attendants, smiling.

"It's Oscar Wilde."

He wrote the name on the green board.

I wondered who this person was and how a Chinese poet from the
Tang dynasty could have anything to do with a Westerner.

"They excelled in using symbols or images to express themselves in
their poems and writings."

The speaker elaborated further:

"For instance, in this poem, Li Shangyin says, 'Eastern winds weaken…'
which implies that his time – the late Tang – is not as grand and robust
as mid-Tang."

He went on:

"The poets in mid-Tang, such as Li Bai, write, 'The wind blows over thousands of miles. It reaches the strategic Yumen Pass and far beyond.' These two different wind expressions reveal the distinct difference between the time and its destiny behind these two poets."

My mind floated between understanding and un-understanding.

But one thing was apparent: The speaker's illustration lit up something in my brain; such enlightenment sent warmth to my body, and the heat transformed into a sense of blissfulness that embraced me.

Just as quickly, though, I shook off the happiness and suppressed the smile that started to emerge on my face. A sense of unworthiness attacked me.

Lowering my body, I pillowed my head on my arms on the table. But, I could not stop myself from looking up as I did not want to lose sight of the speaker.

Like my younger self, who found refuge in books, this speaker and his talk revived the younger, purer me.

"Apart from the weakened eastern wind, Li Shangyin says, 'The silkworm will only stop weaving when it passes away, and the candle will only stop weeping when it burns out.' Li uses these two images to elaborate on life conditions. Each one of us can be a silkworm; each one of us can be a candle. The poet might be poking us to contemplate what we love, may it be a person, may it be an object. Whether such a human being or thing has meaning is not the most critical issue. Instead, it is during the process of our love that we give it all."

He paused and looked at us.

"It is not that we do the thing for others. We do it purely for ourselves. We do it to complete our lives. These two verses touch many people because they are about acknowledging life, and more specifically, about living out our life's passion."

I could not grasp the meaning of his explanations then, but I cherished his words and imprinted them on my mind.

"Similarly, the English writer Oscar Wilde, in his *The Nightingale and the Rose,* writes about a university student who falls in love with a girl.

The girl tells the boy she will only dance with him when he brings her a red rose. But in his garden, the boy can't find any roses, let alone a red one. He cries. A nightingale hears his cry. She feels the boy's love and sadness and decides to help fulfill the boy's wish. So, she presses her breast against a thorn and starts to sing. Her blood pours into the veins of the tree. Overnight, a rose begins to bloom, and when its petals unfold, they are so bright and red."

The speaker's eyes swept around. He continued.

"Wilde uses symbolism to describe that if we are willing to give it all, including our lives, some beautiful miracles may grow out of the endeavor."

He paused again, then proceeded.

"The next morning, the boy opens his window and finds an amazing red rose that appears right before his eyes. But he doesn't see that the body of the nightingale lies still underneath the red rose. As you may know, literary symbolism is when we use a fairy tale or an allusion to illustrate an individual's life experience."

The lecture hall fell into a deep silence. I could almost hear the high-pitched yet stunning singing of the nightingale from afar.

My eyes were glued to the words on the green board:

"The untitled poem by Li Shangyin. *The Nightingale and the Rose* by Oscar Wilde."

The imagery of the silkworm, the candle, the nightingale, and the red rose danced in my head. They spun round and round, transporting me far and beyond.

The nightingale's singing continued to reverberate inside my mind, reminding me how devoted the nightingale was as she gave up her life for what she believed.

Daiyu from *Dream of the Red Chamber* cried a lot because the crying was what she came to this world for, to return tears (water) to Baoyu. The tears were her thanks to Baoyu (a rock), who watered her (a plant) in their previous life. When she finished returning her tears, she was free and gone.

I wondered if I shared the same fate with Daiyu. Maybe I also owed my mother water from our former life, and I came to this world to settle this debt with her through weeping because of her.

The thought shocked me. I got up and sneaked out.

I did not notice the guest speaker's name that day, and it was impossible to find out who he was at the time of writing this. But the speaker might have been Professor Chiang Hsun, a renowned Taiwanese writer, poet, and painter, as I read some of his books later and found content similar to this talk.

Goodbye to Jizhou

I had not forgotten my intention to join a secondary school in Taiwan. When I stayed with the student union, the vice-president Jizhou or president Yusheng would take me to visit different Taipei City districts whenever they had the time. We knocked on some secondary school doors and asked if they could admit me as a student.

But the answer was always the same: They could not accept me.

To these schools, I was no different from a Western student. Therefore, I needed to apply from my "home" country and obtain admission to a Taiwanese school and a Taiwanese student visa before going to Taiwan.

Jizhou and Yusheng thought that Taipei might be stricter as it was the capital of Taiwan. They made inquiries with other students to see if someone had friends in Taichung (a municipality on the western side of central Taiwan) who could help me there.

Soon enough, they found some connections in Taichung and it became my next destination.

When it was time to leave, Jizhou took me to Taipei Main Station to catch a Taichung train. The night before, he gave me a student contact from Tunghai University and told me that the person would come and pick me up from the train station upon my arrival.

The train ticket Jizhou bought for me was for the train to depart around noon.

When we got to the station, he went to a kiosk and bought a lunch box.

Then he led me into the train, found the seat, put the lunch box on top of the folding table in front, and put my luggage – the little belongings

I had – on the overhead rack. Seeing that everything was well set, he turned to leave.

I panicked and followed him.

But I stopped myself at the door.

He stepped outside the train.

I gripped the train's door frame.

A faint faith grew in my head, telling me I needed to get going. I should not grow comfortable relying on Jizhou, Yusheng, and other wondrous students I had met at National Taiwan University.

Jizhou lowered his body, looked me in the eyes, and said:

"Fongling, I don't know what you are running away from. I don't know if it's right for me to help you keep running."

Doubts and concerns crowded his eyes.

"But I do know that's what you want to do. And you seem to have some ideas about what you are searching for on this journey."

Resolution in his voice took over.

"So I decided to help you. I believe our paths have crossed for good reasons."

He gave me a nod, adding weight to his words.

"Now our ways are separating. It would be best if you moved on. Good luck. Stay safe."

Tears blurred my eyes.

I could not find any words to thank him enough.

I looked at him helplessly.

He smiled and nodded in acknowledgment.

I stepped back before the door was closed.

He remained standing.

I ran to my seat, watching out for him through the window.

He gave me a wave.

The train was ready to depart.

Our eyes locked for the last time.

I looked away, letting him go.

Somewhere afar, plum flowers blossomed in the hue of bright purplish pink, basking in the most welcome wintry mid-day sunshine.

The well-rooted plum groves were thriving. They flowered and fruited in places they belonged. Such confidence contributed to the healthy blossoms, making them proud and happy amidst the foliage.

The intense fragrance of the plum blossoms was the fragrance of their self-knowledge and self-value. They knew who they were.

Fong, fragrance, is part of my name. Yet, I did not know what my fragrance was.

I envied them, envied their certainty.

Then I saw some cosmos flowers in the stone pots on the platform, drifting in the wind.

When the train began moving, its current blew off a few cosmos flowers.

The rootless flowers floated around for a fleeting moment. Then they dropped suddenly into the gap between the platform and the train.

The Cultural City

My train entered Taichung Station. Standing outside the station, I looked back at its architecture.

The vastness of the building was breathtaking, with its brick walls and high ceilings.

The central bell tower, dressed in copper sheets, had a pointed roof.

Below the gable, a sizable arcaded window was embedded and embellished with elaborate ornamental beams and columns.

There must be endless scenes witnessed by the station and many desires recorded in its ample interior spaces as southern Taiwanese moved up north to find jobs, hoping for a better life.

"Fongling?"

A voice jolted me back to the moment.

Realizing the sound came from behind me, I quickly turned and answered:

"Yes, I am. You must be Hsinmei?"

"Yes, this is she. Welcome to Taichung!"

Hsinmei was a round-faced, shoulder-length-haired young woman.

She smiled, radiating self-assurance and geniality.

She stepped forward and extended her hand to me.

We shook hands, firmly – Hsinmei's style.

Hsinmei led me to the place where she parked her scooter. As we walked, she told me she would take me back to her university dormitory, where she had a bed.

Feeling blessed and grateful, I thanked her profusely.

She told me it was her pleasure and gave me her gorgeous smile. It put me at ease straight away. She handed me a helmet, and we were soon on the road.

Taichung means "middle of Taiwan." To its north is Taipei, and to its south is Tainan. Being in the middle allowed Taichung to meld the arts from the two diverse cities.

This central point of the island, Taichung, evolved over time into a cultural city in its own right as it encapsulated the essence of the island's fine arts. The place also passionately promoted the artists and writers who chose to live there.

As I was sitting behind Hsinmei, she told me we were riding on Zhongzheng Road. We passed by quite a few bookstores. Hsinmei told me there used to be more: Zhong Yang Bookstore, Han Nui Bookstore, The Regent Store – all of which had existed on this road – were scattered around the city now.

Also, I found the roads in Taichung were broader than in Taipei. Our scooter seemed so small and free-running among few cars. The sense of tightness that often held me hostage loosened its grip.

I put my hands lightly on the waist of Hsinmei. After a while, it felt like we were old friends, and this was another outing of ours.

Tunghai University (THU), where Hsinmei studied, was the first private Christian university in Taiwan. It has a picturesque campus and several landmarks.

Architecture masters I.M. Pei and C.K. Chen designed the famous Luce Chapel, Tunghai's most visited landmark.

Besides the chapel, other scenic spots inside THU included the campus mall, Tunghai Lake, traditional Chinese-style buildings, and the spacious Tunghai farm.

Hsinmei, a devoted Christian, organized Bible study every Wednesday night and attended Sunday services. Soon, she invited me to all these events.

I restarted my learning of English by studying the Bible.

Hsinmei gave me a pocket-size bilingual Bible as a present.

I put it next to my pillow as I had done with my beloved diary.

The Bible became my companion for the rest of the trip to Taiwan.

I tried to apply the vocabulary I learned from the Bible to my life. This way, I could memorize the new words and make them mine.

For instance, I met these words then: omnipotent and omnipresent. The sentences or thoughts I came up with to remember these words were: My parents' influence over me was omnipotent and omnipresent. Even though I had run away from home, far away from them, still, I could not escape their impact. I was angry, melancholic, and helpless, just like them.

This realization shook me.

One of the main reasons I ran away from home and Hong Kong was to be as far from the old events and influences as possible and learn a new way of living, one with hope. But this discovery that I might never be able to change for the better and grow out of my negative thoughts infuriated me, making me feel powerless all over again.

I turned to literature once more to seek consolation.

Independent bookstores in Taichung City became my new sanctuary. And amazingly, literature occupied most of the shelves of the many bookshops I frequented.

Central Bookstore, my favorite, had a classical, elegant look. Works of literature lined its second floor's shelves. I selected a few books, went to the deepest corner, and read to my heart's content. It was like I had reverted to the twelve- or thirteen-year-old me who hid and read in the second-floor book corner of my primary school in Hong Kong.

My readings taught me that old Taiwanese literature focused on the traditional poetry style inherited from the Tang and Song dynasties. Many poetry clubs or groups flourished then as poets regularly discussed and recited poems.

However, during the Japanese occupation (1895-1945), Taiwan began to develop a distinct style of literature. From the outset, the movement focused on multilingual development. In addition to Chinese works, the evolution encouraged Japanese and Taiwanese writings. Social and political forces also propelled the island's literary advancement.

When I learned about the Taiwanese new literature progression, I thought about the May 4th Movement in mainland China. Without delving too deep, I started to gather information about May 4th to understand better the two movements, which echoed each other.

May 4th – a Chinese intellectual revolution and sociopolitical reform campaign in 1917-21 – had a key figure: Hu Shih.

Then, I encountered Hu's poem, *Butterfly*.

> Two yellow butterflies, both flew to the sky.
> Without knowing why, one of them suddenly died.

That was my translation of the opening of his poem, which marked the beginning of contemporary Chinese poetry. The simple language of the verse reflected Hu's dream of popularizing the vernacular, making Chinese accessible to the general public rather than limiting its practice and appreciation inside ivory towers.

The validation of vernacular Chinese prompted free thinking. This was one of Hu's astonishing achievements, considering he was an exceptional scholar of the classics. He challenged tradition and resisted authority, becoming one of the most remarkable intellectuals of the 20th century.

I wondered why my mother never mentioned Hu. Soon, I found out that he was a non-believer in Communism. When the party established the PRC on the mainland in 1949, Hu left for Taiwan and the USA.

Later, I also discovered that unlike Mother's favorite writer, Lu Xun, Hu had a gentle mien. But Hu was passionate, too. With his profound knowledge in vast fields and refined manner, his lectures at Beijing University and elsewhere were always filled with abundant ardent admirers.

Hu was also a phenomenally prolific writer. His forty-four books and countless articles have influenced innumerable Chinese worldwide from that time until now. I was so proud to become one such.

Apart from reforming the language, Hu advocated the idea of modernizing China through science and democracy. Invited by Chiang Kai-Shek, Hu led the Academia Sinica on Taiwan. In the 1950s, he published *Free China*, a magazine of monumental significance, as later scholars regarded it as the second May 4th Movement.

Free China seeded science and democracy – the two pivotal pursuits of the movement – on the island's rich soil, where they blossomed.

A Taiwanese writer I appreciated during the island's new literature progression period was Wu Zhuoliu. The book that made Wu's name was *Orphan of Asia,* which he completed in 1945.

Born in Japanese-occupied Taiwan, raised in the scholarly traditions of ancient China by his grandfather but forced into the Japanese educational system, Taiming Hu, the protagonist of *Orphan of Asia*, ultimately finds himself estranged from all three cultures.

This book can be read as Wu's autobiographical novel. The literati consider it a classic of modern Asian literature and a groundbreaking expression of the postwar Taiwanese national consciousness.

Wu wrote the book in Japanese. I read its translated version in Chinese.

Hu, the protagonist of *Orphan*, spoke to me a great deal. I did not have any attachment to mainland China, where I was born, Hong Kong, where I subsequently immigrated with my family and grew up, or Taiwan, where I arrived on a tourist visa. Like Hu, I was in between, living my life in transit.

I continued to explore Taiwan's literary development.

After the Japanese occupation, the island's writing focused on using Chinese as its creative tool. Hence, modern or new Chinese literature in Taiwan bloomed in the 60s and 70s.

A poet named Chouyu Zheng caught my attention. His most famous poem is *A Mistake*.

> The tapping sound of my hoof is a beautiful mistake
> I am not a homecomer but only a passer-by.
> (My translation)

Thus ends *A Mistake*.

It looks like a poignant love poem on the surface as it describes a woman hoping in vain for the return of her lover. But after digging deeper, I found that this poem was about war, or anti-war to be more precise.

Zheng spent most of his young life traveling with his high-ranking Nationalist military officer father during the civil war era in mainland China. A horse nearly ran him over on a narrow street in a small town when his family was in exile.

Therefore, the hooves' scary tapping sound was indelibly imprinted on his mind. The sound also found its way into many of his poems, especially this one.

A Mistake is cloaked in a shroud of longing and hoping.

The poem opened the door into Zheng's world.

I read many of his commentaries. His idea of poetic sentiments fascinated me.

Zheng stated that a poet needed to possess two kinds of sentiments. One was the poet's passion for her country, the nation, humanity, and the environment. This notion usually stemmed from the macro point of view. The other sentiments he referred to were the emotions arising from family and friends and between lovers.

He also reckoned that a poet should contemplate life by asking many questions. For instance, she should question why and how certain events took place.

Zheng said he could not emphasize enough the importance of developing an interest in everyday life.

He also explained that possessing poetic sentiments was necessary but insufficient for writing a compelling poem. A poet should refine her lyrical skills through guidance-seeking and practicing. Only through incessant writing, revising, and reflecting could a pearly poem be born.

He revealed that the trigger to write often seemed to arrive at one's doorstep naturally. But if we exposed ourselves to different facets of life, we would have more chances to have the trigger that sparked something in our hearts and caused us to compose.

His words inspired me and gave me hope.

I did not think I could be a poet, but I knew I possessed those sentiments and asked many questions. Perhaps I could be a prose writer.

Furthermore, now that I had faced many uncertainties and exposed myself to different life facets, I should pick up my pen again and write.

Then I remembered that I used to compose Chinese *ci* lyrics. A new one came to me.

My Olive Tree
When I'm in my adopted city
People often ask if I am a local
Part of me wants to say, yes, I am
Part of me feels no, I am not

When I go to my hometown
People also ask if I am a local

Part of me wants to say, yes, I am
Part of me feels no, I am not

I belong neither here nor there
Not being grounded is frightening
Yet, it liberates
Freeing me to seek my olive tree

And then, I encountered Walis Nokan, an Atayal writer originally from the Mihuo tribe located on a mountain in north-central Taiwan.

Walis Nokan's collection of essays, entitled *Eternal Village*, was published in 1990. It broadened my horizons.

Under the city's sky
the mountainous migrant birds lined the steel beams
displaying the migrants' original wilderness, beauty
Young villagers cry
Disappearing into the darkness of the urban high-rises
They've been the treasures and future of their villages
But now, each of them has been untethered, uprooted.
(My translation)

These are the words printed at the back of the book that gripped me.

I finished reading the book and learned that there was another angle to looking at things.

After the civil war, the Han Chinese, who emigrated to Taiwan in hordes, rapidly developed the island and destroyed many natural environments. They committed acts of destruction in the name of development, civilization, and progress.

To the tribal people, who had been there much earlier, living in harmony with nature, the "development" by the Han Chinese demolished their homes, forcing them into permanent exile and living in abject poverty for the rest of their lives.

The sixteen-year-old me could not comprehend the magnitude of the problem. But Walis Nokan's authentic, deep, heart-wrenching voice penetrated me.

His urgent voice urged me to open my eyes and see different perspectives from different people's points of view.

Walis Nokan also inspired me to create more space in my head and always have a place to receive and process alternative, weaker, marginal messages.

When I reread his works later in my life, I found they echoed Albert Camus's idea, "Those of us who can speak have a responsibility to say something for those of us who can't."

Hsinmei took me to large and small secondary schools in Taichung to try to find a school that would accept me as a student. But no such luck.

After nearly half a year of searching, knocking, and being rejected for the same reason as in Taipei – I needed to apply from Hong Kong – Hsinmei still would not give up.

She went on to contact a friend of hers. Her friend studied at National Cheng Kung University in Tainan, southern Taiwan, and told her about me. Her friend immediately agreed to help.

With Hsinmei's full support, I would soon embark on a journey to Tainan.

During my final evening in Taichung, Hsinmei took me to explore Fengjia.

The famous Fengjia Night Market was inside Feng Chia University. The goods were trendy and affordable as they catered to students. The market spanned Wen Hua Night Market, Fengjia Road, Fuxing Road, and Xitun Road.

There was no established entrance, but as a tip, Hsinmei told me that the university gate would be the landmark. All the stalls and stores shoot

off the alleys and streets on practically all corners. She asked me to wait
for her at the gate if we were separated.

Fengjia, bustling, had motorcycles springing out from all directions. I
stayed vigilant. But no matter how carefully I walked, keeping to myself,
I rubbed elbows with other visitors all the time.

Hsinmei bought me a wide and wild range of food: stinky tofu, hot and
spicy diced chicken, pork cutlets, sugar-glazed fruit sticks, golden fried
squid, egg cakes, oyster omelets, grilled prawns, scallops, grilled sausages,
and bubble milk tea, which is said to have originated from Taichung.

We sat on a roadside bench, indulging ourselves with the delectable
goodies.

At some point, Hsinmei put down her disposable chopsticks, turned
to me, and said:

"Fongling, I can't help you to realize your dream and get you settled in
Taichung. But I want to fill your stomach with our gourmet treats, our
specialties."

She looked at me warmly and went on:

"Whenever you touch your belly, I hope you will recall with relish
that plenty of fantastic foods and books are awaiting you at the heart of
Taiwan."

She paused. Our eyes met.

She said: "Please, do come back anytime as you wish."

I eagerly nodded as words choked in my throat.

We sat still, enjoying each other's company.

Right there and then, I remembered that she had never pushed me to
become a Christian, nor did she get upset with me for not accepting her
religion or stop helping me. The vastness of her heart and the kindness of
her soul touched me much more than religion ever did.

I saluted Hsinmei and loved her like my sister.

When it was time for me to leave, Hsinmei and I hugged for a long time
on the station platform.

Finally, she let go of me, and I entered the train. After finding my window seat, I held up the pocket-size bilingual Bible, waving her goodbye.

As the train started departing, I waved more frantically, keeping at it until she became a small spot on the platform.

Feeling low about yet another separation, I did not register any views during the train journey. However, from time to time, the memory returned of my arrival at Taichung, with the station's red-brick walls and the bronze bell sitting proudly atop the building. These images lived on, encouraging me.

I am not a homecomer but only a passer-by.

The closing line of Zheng's poem, *A Mistake*, jumped into my head.

It was very doubtful that I would or could become a homecomer either.

Like the poem's speaker, I might be a passer-by for the rest of my life.

The Phoenix City

Tainan Railway Station is an old white building. The station has adopted an eclectic Western or colonial style and is well-aged by the tropical sun. But it must have seen its glory days when the building was modern and chic.

The site has over one hundred years of history, dating back to the beginning of the north-south rail system in Taiwan.

The station's current form is the second generation, built during the Japanese occupation and completed in 1936. Its modern style was part of the progressive building the Japanese were doing in Tainan.

The building used to have a hotel, a restaurant, a bar, and recreation areas. These amenities were all history now.

I learned this from the information leaflet I picked up at the station when I got off the train. It also said that the railway divided the city into east and west.

The rear entrance was to the east and accessed National Cheng Kung University, the Far Eastern Department Store, and Shangri-la's Far Eastern Hotel. The front entrance led to downtown.

Someone was running toward me from the rear entrance.

As she approached, I found that she was boyishly good-looking with a head of short hair, sporty attire, sharp and ebullient.

"Hi, are you Fongling?

"Yes, I am. Hi!"

"I'm Sihua Li. Sorry, I'm late!"

"Oh, that's okay. Sihua, thank you so much for coming and being willing to help!"

"Ah, it's my pleasure!" She ran her fingers through her hair and blushed.

Sihua was Hsinmei's secondary school friend.

Hsinmei told me that she had come to live with her grandmother in Tainan when her parents went through a dreadful divorce. She thought she was close to both of her parents. But after they announced their separation, they became strangers to Hsinmei as she had never seen them behave so cruelly.

Deeply depressed, Hsinmei felt that everything around her had turned dark and strange and that nothing made sense. Luckily, her grandma, the sunshine, and Sihua in Tainan came to her rescue. They restored her faith in life when her world collapsed.

Hsinmei firmly believed that Tainan and Sihua would also work their magic on me.

"Okay, Fongling, let's get going."

Sihua's voice sounded like wind chimes made of small, light pieces of glass – plinking – so musical and enchanting.

We walked, talked, and laughed on our way toward National Cheng Kung University.

National Cheng Kung University was impressive in many ways.

Cheng Kung had ten campuses, one hundred and eighty hectares in total area, making it one of the most spacious universities on the island then. Also, the campuses were green and beautiful.

Contrary to Tunghai, which was small and focused on art and humanities, Cheng Kung was grand and well-known for its science and technology topics.

The buildings in Tunghai were old and traditional; their counterparts in Cheng Kung were modern, with state-of-the-art solar energy-saving systems built atop many buildings.

Sihua majored in engineering. She led me onto Shengli Campus, where her dormitory, number three, was located.

When we got there, Sihua pointed out that the old library compound was also on this campus but in the northeastern section. The front of the library became a venue for students to engage in self-study.

At its rear, a building housed the Alumni Information Center, the Cheng Kung Incubation Center, and a campus co-op store. The northwestern section had Zenda Suite, a hotel complex for Cheng Kung alums. In this campus's southwest, you would find the university's swimming pool.

I could not wait to explore all these places, especially the library.

One day, I ventured into another campus called Kuangfu.

The boulevard had double rows of trees planted along its sides, making it a compelling campus walk. I strolled along the road, passing the university administrative building, other academic houses, and more dormitories.

A student activity center, basketball courts, volleyball courts, and tennis courts came one after another. Around the Chiang Kai-Shek Gymnasium, many student activities were happening simultaneously.

Effervescent energy infused the campus. My feet became lighter, and my pace faster.

In the center, surrounded by the Department of History, the Department of Chinese Literature, and the Department of Foreign Languages and Literature, was Cheng Kung Lake.

The greenery encircling the pond gave it a great sense of liveliness. A red bridge crossed the lake. It was like a Chinese saying, "*hua long dian jing*," bringing the painted dragon to life by adding the pupils to its eyes.

The short red wooden bridge created a sensational finishing touch to this serene scenic site, making it a wondrous place to walk, ponder, and discover.

Then, a gigantic Banyan tree appeared.

The Banyan tree trunk might take up to fifty grown-ups stretching their arms to circle it.

Many individual students or professors, pairs of lovers, friends, and families read, played, talked, or sat under the shade of this enormous tree.

This Banyan's large, leathery, glossy, green, and elliptical leaves acted like great loyal companions protecting the blessed souls underneath them.

I sat upon one of the aerial prop roots that matured into thick, woody trunks.

Soon, I began dreaming about becoming a student and being rooted like this Banyan.

I hoped to grow to my full potential as this tree had done for itself.

May the richness of the soil and the greatness of people's hearts nourish me and help me become another Banyan, standing tall and proud, taking up space. Unapologetically.

One day, Sihua invited me to her home to meet her family.

We got on her scooter, and off we went.

While the pace and atmosphere of Taipei, the current capital of Taiwan, were fast, mercantile, and hard-edged, Tainan, the old capital, was slower, cultured, and reflective.

People said the contrast was like Tokyo and Kyoto. But I could not confirm that since I had not been to Japan.

Sitting on the back seat of Sihua's scooter, feeling safe and sound, I proceeded to admire this ancient city and the transformation it was going through.

Tainan was the place where Taiwanese history began.

The Netherlands ruled Tainan in the seventeenth century. Then, China besieged the city during the Qing dynasty and governed it from the late seventeenth to the nineteenth century.

Japan followed and controlled it from 1895 to 1945. The buildings reflecting the colonial days survived.

Embracing that history, Tainan developed into a city with its own character and chicness.

And it dawned on me that the Taiwanese's development of their own regional identity might start from Tainan.

The city had risen to prominence as a place where Taiwanese could reclaim their roots and look for "the real Taiwan."

We arrived at Sihua's home.

A three-story concrete building, Sihua's home was situated in one of the charming alleys in parts of Tainan that the wave of redevelopment had left untouched.

The house's first floor featured a living room, dining room, kitchen, and toilet. The second level had the bedrooms of Sihua and her brother, who was performing military service. Her father's study room and her parents' master bedroom were on the top floor.

Sihua's father, a retired army officer, was tall, tanned, and handsome. Now I knew where Sihua got her boyish good looks.

Daddy Li kept his posture – sitting or standing – upright.

Sihua, on the contrary, moved with ease.

Mommy Li's almond-shaped eyes shone exquisitely with wisdom. Her dainty body and caring, soft voice drew one immediately to her.

Upon arrival, Mommy Li brought us two bowls of sizzling beef soup, the Tainanese's breakfast. It had vermilion beef strips and other goodies in it. We took it as our late breakfast.

I cradled my bowl of soup and stared into it for a long moment.

It was heart-warming and aromatic. The soup's steam curled upwards into my nostrils, clearing some space in my sinuses.

Then, Mommy Li busied herself with preparing lunch.

Daddy Li sat down with us and began chatting.

Once Daddy Li learned I loved literature, he said he would be back soon. He climbed the steps two at a time.

Sihua's eyes met mine – we smiled at each other quizzically.

She whispered that she had never seen her father so enthusiastic and talkative.

"Look, here!"

Daddy Li ran down the steps and waved a book in our direction.

I could neither see the book title nor the author's name.

He hastened toward us.

Sihua and I quickly emptied the space between us for him.

He sat and showed the book to me, and I passed it on to Sihua.

It was a poetry collection by Yu Kwangchung.

Daddy Li held the book again and told us that Yu was the poet most read and loved by the older soldiers and workers of the Nationalist Government who fled to Taiwan after the Chinese Civil War.

He reckoned that those soldiers and government workers felt that Yu's poetry since the 1970s focused on the theme of nostalgia for China.

> When I was small, nostalgia was a tiny postage stamp
> I, on this shore, my mother, on the other
> When I grew up, nostalgia was a boat ticket
> I, on this end, my bride on the opposite.
> (My translation)

Daddy Li recited the beginning of Yu's poem, *Nostalgia*.

He went on and said:

"My father was not one of the soldiers who escaped to Taiwan with Chiang Kai-Shek. Father had come with other fishers and settled on this island long ago. But my father still considered himself Chinese and often talked about returning to his village as he yearned to visit his ancestral house, his roots."

Daddy Li gave a meaningful look to Sihua and then to me.

"It is very different from Sihua's generation now. Her classmates and most youngsters these days see themselves as Taiwanese."

Neither accusation nor criticism could be traced in his voice, though perhaps resignation. He went on.

"I was born in Taiwan. But I learned from my father that our family's homeland is Yongchun county in Fujian province, just like this poet Yu."

"Yongchun?" I asked and quickly added: "My parents' hometown, Nan'an, is only about an hour away from there!"

"Wow, that's wonderful. You must tell me more."

Daddy Li's eyes were full of great expectations.

I rapidly replied:

"Sorry, I couldn't tell you much about it. I'd only passed there a few times when I was very young. Those times happened when my parents took our family from their workplaces back to Nan'an for Chinese New Year celebrations."

I looked at Daddy Li, apologetically.

He shook his head and gave me an encouraging, bright smile. I continued.

"My mother told us once that Yongchun had high-quality wood, and the people there used it to build a bridge called... ah, Dongguan Bridge. Mother said legend has it that the bridge had lasted eight hundred years!"

Daddy Li seemed euphoric. His eyes sparkled, maybe dreaming about walking on the bridge with his father and other relatives.

I was proud of myself for a change.

"Come, let's have a simple lunch." Mommy Li called out.

We entered the dining room, and I was awestruck.

Mommy Li had prepared a banquet.

I looked to Sihua. She shrugged and mouthed: "That's Mom."

Mommy Li prepared:

Dragon beard vegetable salad drizzled with homemade sesame sauce, stir-fried long beans, omelet with *chye-poh*, pickles, milkfish simmered in ginger vinaigrette, braised pork belly with preserved cabbage, Taiwanese style spring rolls, clear radish with pork ribs soup, and steaming fragrant rice.

Mommy Li asked us to dig in and eat up.

My admiration for her food cheered her no end. Merrily, she said:

"Taiwanese cooking is simple, since the 1950s and 1960s without the influence of the fancy Western cooking or modern fusion styles."

The raw dragon beard in the salad was sweet and crunchy. The foods that emerged from the wok included the piquant and crisp beans, the tasty omelet, the silky milkfish, and the succulent, flavorsome braised pork.

I could not put down my chopsticks.

Still, I paid attention to Mommy Li's words, nodding my head frequently in response.

The more I reveled in her food and talk, the merrier she became.

High-spiritedly, Mommy Li proceeded to tell me more about Tainan.

"You see, Tainan was redesigned by the Japanese in the late nineteenth century, bombed to pieces by the Americans in the mid-twentieth, and rebuilt in a frenzy of economic growth."

She looked sad and serious for a moment, then returned to her cheery self and went on.

"It's not the prettiest city on the island. But we restored many historical sites, such as the oldest and most important Confucian temple, among many more Buddhist and Taoist temples around the town."

She was positively beaming with pleasure.

"Yes, Mommy Li," I said. "Sihua has taken me to visit many of those."

Mommy Li smiled at Sihua and me approvingly. She continued.

"Also, we are reviving some old landmarks, such as the Hayashi Department Store and the building that used to house the Tainan Prefectural Government, to turn them into useful, educational places."

She paused for a second and said: "Tainan hence gained its nickname – a phoenix city."

I felt so blessed to receive so much good food for my body and brain.

*

After the meal, Sihua helped Mommy Li to clean up. I offered my help, but they would not hear of it.

Daddy Li told me it was okay and led me back to the living room.

He brought some homemade tea with kumquat, chrysanthemum, rock sugar, dried pineapple, and candied melon. Daddy Li started making the tea in a fine porcelain pot. When he finished, he sat back, leaving the tea to simmer. After a while, he served it to me.

We sipped at our teas.

Daddy Li reiterated his wish to visit his ancestral homeland and told me it was surreal and joyous for him to meet me, someone from a place close to his roots.

"My wife is right – Tainan, or the whole of Taiwan, has been developing speedily. The older generation suffers from collective amnesia while their offspring strive to disown their origin and sever all ancestral links."

He let out a deep sigh.

"What's the point of it moving forward but disregarding its history, its roots?"

He added: "Taiwan is an island; the roots can't grow deep. And without being rooted, I'm not sure where it will drift to."

His words encouraged me to consider the issue further.

If Taiwan were a boat, its passengers' aspirations would be similar to mine. The ambition might be to break free and sail off. Yet others could wish to return to the harbor for safety. To be anchored felt good.

No matter what we chose, the passengers and I could not deny or escape the influence of our shared culture, such as Confucian teaching, Mandarin or Hokkien for speaking, and traditional Chinese characters for writing.

I pondered the history. Taiwan encapsulated some of the best essence of Chinese culture as it evaded the Cultural Revolution.

In my teenaged mind then, I hoped that this boat called Taiwan, its passengers, and I dreamed the same dreams: to sail off, discover our courage and abilities through the voyage, and then reach the foreign land, learn from it, return, and enrich our motherland with both our authentic and learned selves.

Hua Mulan, the woman warrior who came to mind during my flight to Taipei, returned. I realized then that even though I was seeking a new identity, I was still rooted in Chinese culture.

I smiled and looked at Daddy Li.

He continued. "When Sihua's brother returns from military service, I will take my family back to visit Yongchun."

His eyes filled with determination.

"I regret not doing it earlier when my father was still alive."

And he added quickly: "I don't want to have a second regret of not visiting it myself with my family."

We both sat and got lost in our thoughts.

The gentle exchanges between Mommy Li and Sihua embraced us.

It was time for Sihua and me to leave.

All four of us stood in front of the house and said our goodbyes.

Mommy Li gave me a jar of her homemade sesame sauce and one of pickles.

Daddy Li gifted me with the poem collection of Yu Kwangchung.

I held these precious presents to my chest, making eye contact with the members of this beautiful family one by one.

Tears began sliding down my face.

I did not know how to express my tremendous gratitude toward them.

Through my teary eyes, I gazed at them helplessly.

Mommy and Daddy Li smiled and nodded as I saw tears emerging from their eyes.

Then, Mommy Li stepped forward, drew me into her, and wrapped her arms around me.

Daddy Li followed.

He walked closer and encircled both of us in his embrace. I had never experienced that with my parents.

Tears kept rushing out. But I forced them back. I should not raise concerns or worries for these singularly kind and loving people.

It was as if Sihua could read my mind.

She stepped forward, gently reminding her parents that she needed to attend a project meeting that evening and I had part-time work to do. So we should get going.

Her parents nodded but did not let go.

Softly, Sihua reached for me, took the things from me, and put them into a bag.

She then put an arm around my shoulder and led me away.

As we arrived at the alley's exit, I looked back.

Her parents were two statues of guardian angels.

I gave them a wave and quickly averted my gaze.

Every cell in my body told me to run back to them.

One day, when I finished my part-time work at a café near the Kuangfu campus, I took a walk and arrived at the garden of that majestic Banyan.

Sitting upon an aerial prop root, I started to contemplate the trees.

How good it was to be a tree. It stood there for eternity and did not have any posture displaying melancholy.

Most of its roots penetrated deep into the ground, safe and sound.

Its upper body swung with the wind.

Some of its leaves scattered in the shadows while others sunbathed.

I admired its quietness, its self-possession. Each independent tree personified *gu du*, solitude, one of my favorite words.

> Don't ask me where I come from
> My hometown is far away
> …

A young lady's singing voice and guitar sound jolted me out of my reverie.

She played and sang *The Olive Tree* – the song that liberated me and led me to Taiwan.

When the young woman finished singing, I approached her and asked who had written the lyrics. I only knew its singer.

"Why, it's Sanmao, the great wandering writer from Taiwan."

Then she said:

"What a tragedy – she committed suicide last year!"

Shocked, I became speechless.

She went on.

"We are organizing a concert with readings of her prose and poems. We want to commemorate her, to celebrate her extraordinary life. You are welcome to join too!"

She wrote down the concert's details on a small piece of paper and handed it to me.

I thanked the young woman and walked away.

My feet were laden with shock and sorrow.

Then, I found myself walking toward a bookshop outside the campus.

On the bookshop's third floor, it featured literary books.

I located the works of Sanmao straight away.

Immediately, I dived into her world, losing myself in her books.

The Stories of the Sahara. My first one.

The next day, I returned to the same bookshop and the same corner.

I devoured her *Gone with the Rainy Season*.

Sanmao was the pen name of Chen Ping, a courageous and glamorous globe-trotting writer who had published twenty books in Chinese based on her experiences traveling across Europe and Africa. The journeys ranged from the 1970s to her death in 1991.

She was essentially self-taught from the age of twelve and plunged herself into the literary world by reading. She read works by contemporary Chinese writers such as Lu Xun, Ba Jin, and Bing Xin. Other renowned international literary works, such as *The Count of Monte Cristo*, *Don Quixote de la Mancha*, and *Gone with the Wind*, were among her favorites.

Sanmao declared her greatest love to be *Dream of the Red Chamber*.

Upon learning the similarities in our characters and admiration for specific writers and books, I became a faithful fan of Sanmao.

Then and there, I realized the time had come for me to end these wanderings in Taiwan. Even though Sanmao was primarily self-taught, she did go to university. She studied first at the Chinese Culture University in Taiwan and subsequently at the University of Madrid in Spain.

Despite Sihua's continuous efforts to get me into a school in Tainan, it was impossible. I had to return to Hong Kong for my studies to proceed.

Being a university student, traveling worldwide, and writing like Sanmao became my dream.

The two years of wandering across Taiwan helped me to rebuild myself.

The people I met and the friends I made through this journey enabled such rebuilding.

The businessman on the plane, the two policemen, Jizhou, Yusheng, Cheer, Hsinmei, Sihua, and her parents – all had woven themselves as important strands into the fabric of my life.

The unconditional love, warmth, and help these wondrous people offered made me believe that I was a decent person worthy of their affection and assistance.

I fell in love with many more outstanding writers and poets in Taiwan, including Pai Hsienyung, Wu Zhuoliu, Zheng Chouyu, Walis Nokan, Yu Kwangchung, and Sanmao. They strengthened my belief in the transformative power of literature.

As a result of this journey, I better understood myself and other human beings through these friends, writers, and poets.

The ache for action – working hard and realizing my dreams – became real and urgent.

I walked into a police station in Tainan and reported myself for overstaying.

The police checked and confirmed that I did not commit any crimes or engage in any illegal activities during my overstay. Then they deported me a week later.

Part Five: Return

Hong Kong

1992 – 1999

Home of Lost Souls

I began living in Chungking Mansions when I turned eighteen in October 1992.

At the end of my two-year journey to Taiwan, the picture of my dreams flashed in my mind. It urged me to return and realize them.

Located at the harbor end of Nathan Road in Tsim Sha Tsui (TST), Chungking Mansions appeared abused. A corridor on the ground floor connected the mansions' five blocks. Together, they became the least favorite children sitting among luxury hotels like the Peninsula and Sheraton; the least favorite like I was among my siblings.

When I first entered Chungking Mansions, a pungent smell – Indian curry mixed with Chinese salted fish – attacked my nostrils. The air on the ground floor was heavy and humid. Standing amid the crowd, I sensed the moisture clinging to my clothes. It felt thick as I breathed it in, coating the inside of my throat.

South Asians, Middle Easterners, and Africans gathered in small groups, conducting business. With my dark complexion, I blended in well. The place brimmed with shops and clamor. I did not mind the noise; I was searching for my voice.

The distance from the entrance to the lift lobby was about one hundred steps. I counted them to keep track. The space in between heaved with men. A slight girl, I braced myself, navigated through the throng, and avoided touching anyone or being touched along the way.

I chose to stay at the Travelers' Lodge Hostel for three reasons. Firstly, it was the cheapest: $45 (US$5.80) per night, while the Imperial Hotel next door was $500 (still relatively inexpensive for a hotel). Secondly, no deposit was required. I paid before noon and had a bed. Lastly, I did not see any Chinese and breathed easier. As a Chinese myself, I knew we could be judgmental.

Travelers' Lodge had a large lobby with a reception desk parallel to the entrance. In the far corner, a bulky TV and a beaten-up sofa took up some space. The foyer bustled with life as an incessant stream of guests arrived and departed. I became almost invisible. It suited me well as I hoped to blend in, a discreet drop in a sea of colors.

The hostel had two rooms with one bed each, a sizable mixed-sex room, and three single-sex rooms with bunk beds. I selected Bed 86, a lower bunk in the women's one, and paid each morning to keep it. Once I forgot to pay on time, and my belongings ended up scattered around the corner next to the rough wooden reception table.

Behind the table sat Marianne, a fortyish Filipina with a menacing face and a high-pitched voice. She wore thick makeup like a mask with a facial expression that mirrored a sullen gray sky. Talking to her could be frightening. You never knew when her anger would rain down on you. I often wondered how the true face of Marianne might have looked before she had become a domestic helper in Hong Kong.

Unfortunately, domestic helpers landed at the bottom of the social hierarchy of Hong Kong. I empathized with the domestic workers as I, an outsider, also tasted the bitterness of discrimination. Whenever I saw Marianne's face, I feared I would grow to be like her, putting on so much makeup to mask my sense of inferiority and insecurity. The veil might seal my mouth, rendering me voiceless.

The other hostel keeper was Cameroon-born Jimmy, in his fifties. Jimmy's voice, deep and dense, sounded like the rumble of distant thunder, matching his slow-moving muscular body. Every other day, Jimmy would inspect each of the guestrooms. His too-long legs were not very coordinated, as one seemed to delay for a second or two before deciding to stride forward in front of the other. But the delay somehow added weight to his inspection.

Marianne and Jimmy were complementary opposites like concave and convex. They got on well and made a great pair of guards, diligently looking after the hostel. Nobody wanted to mess with them. We paid on time.

One night, when I arrived at Chungking Mansions after working at a shop until near midnight, a power failure blacked out my block again. It happened at least once every two months as the illicit hostels mushroomed inside the mansions, initially designed for residential usage.

I pushed through a seedy back door and got to the staircase. As I ascended the stairs to my sixteenth-floor hostel, faint yellow lights from outside crept through the small portholes.

After the rape, my reactions to situations became extreme in strange, unpredictable ways.

It did not concern me if I was in a perilous place like I was now, ascending, alone, a dark staircase infamous for drug dealing and prostitution. But in public places, I often suffered from sudden panic attacks. If anyone accidentally brushed against the bare skin of my arm, I might let out an involuntary scream.

Luckily, I reached my floor safely that night and during the subsequent building blackouts.

Sometime later I made three girlfriends.

Kate, from England, had been there for five months and worked as an English tutor. She was timid and tall, with a tiny mole above her lips, visible only because of her pearly white skin. If I had her skin, my parents might have thought more of me, that I was born superior, a pearl to them, rather than my dark skin that made me look like a peasant's daughter. I stood out from my finer, fairer-skinned sisters and brother.

Julie was a sporty, chirpy Australian. We often walked up Nathan Road to Sham Shui Po to enjoy cheaper meals, during which we talked and laughed louder as people there were not so uptight and pretentious as the ones in TST. Like Julie, I became a jolly visitor. At times, though, I caught a tragic look in her eyes. Maybe that was why we clicked. We both strove to revive the blithe and carefree girls inside ourselves.

Park, a South Korean, was stoutly built and square-faced. The peculiar opacity of Park's dark eyes attested to her private nature. It was unusual for a Korean to travel unaccompanied, let alone a young woman like Park. But she could have said the same about me. Park kept to herself, but when our eyes met at times, I nodded and smiled at her. She always responded in kind. Then she began bidding me goodnight before climbing up to her bunk, and I greeted her when she came down the following morning.

Later on, when I returned from work, I sometimes found sachets of Korean rice crackers or candies next to my pillow. We started conversing in our pidgin English, supplementing it with wild gestures. Using our secret languages, we helped each other connect with the rest.

The mutual acceptance, respect, and bond I developed with Park were things I always longed to have with my sisters.

I loved Park, Julie, and Kate, but when the shared room was full, it felt like the bunk beds, the ceiling, and the walls were closing in on me. There was no window. I crawled into my lower bunk and curled in there like a little trapped mouse.

Then I met three guys: Takeshi, who was Japanese; Ricky, English; and Marcus, German.

Takeshi, a tousle-haired, boyish, good-looking young man with soulful eyes, had a mild stutter. He was like the elder brother I yearned for – so tender and caring.

Ricky was ruggedly handsome with a head of shoulder-length hair that parted in the middle. He often let the strands of his fringe drape down like curtains covering up his face. When he stood close enough for me to feel his warmth, my heart trampolined.

Takeshi and Ricky were in their early twenties.

Marcus, in his thirties, was tall and muscular. Combined with his stern facial expression, he looked intimidating. I kept my distance. But when I heard him speak, his voice was surprisingly sonorous and sincere. It softened his appearance and brought us closer together. But he took drugs and isolated himself from time to time.

Ricky and Marcus had boarded there for many months when I arrived. Their respective lower bunk beds were tightly wrapped with indigo sheets as if they were their most sacred and inviolable property. They existed in their wonderland.

But whenever I needed to speak to Marianne, one of them would appear next to me. Upon seeing Ricky or Marcus, Marianne's face cleared. She listened attentively. And when she replied, her pitch lowered. It worked like magic.

When Park's birthday came, my gang decided to give her a party.

We waited until midnight when the nightwatchman, Jimmy, retreated to his room behind the reception table. Ricky revealed a secret back staircase from our floor to the rooftop of Chungking Mansions. Marcus brought whisky and wine; Takeshi, sake; Park, Korean rice wine; Julie, Kate, Ricky, and I, beers.

When we reached the top of the back staircase, Ricky pushed open a wrought-iron gate. We came out and found a rooftop patio with parapet walls below my waist height. The parapet was broad, about twelve inches wide.

I walked forward, stopped at the front wall, and found flat overhanging eaves that prevented me from seeing Nathan Road right below. Looking out, Peking Road extended exuberantly ahead, the playful neon lights mixed with bar-hoppers, party-goers, and insomniacs conveying the effervescent nightlife of Hong Kong.

The late-night air felt cool, though a sense of humidity mixed with the anxieties of the city clung to one's skin. The heavens stood high, grand, nonchalant. The stars immersed themselves in the striking Hong Kong skyline. This open space contrasted with the low-ceiling, congested hostel down below.

I stared into the wondrous void above and felt my muscles relaxing, letting go of existential fear and concerns. This bigger world was where I belonged. The atmosphere vibrated with my heartbeat, full of vitality. The lightly salted breeze from Victoria Harbour embraced us.

We sat on the ground in the middle of the rooftop yard, forming a circle around the drinks. Marcus held up his lighter, lit it in front of Park, and asked her to make a wish. Park lowered her head, put her palms together in a prayer pose, and did so. We clapped and sang *Happy Birthday*. Her eyes shone; her face glowed. She winked at me before the light went out. I put my arm around her shoulders, and she tilted her head to meet mine. We sat connected and contented.

The drinking and chatting went on. At some point, I gave my left inner thigh a quick pinch, ensuring that I was not dreaming – that I was on top of something for a change. TST, the most glamorous district in the Kowloon peninsula, existed below my feet.

From Datian, "big rice paddy," the prefecture where I was born, to Nan'an, the hometown of my parents, to Hong Kong, then to Taiwan, and now to the top of TST – I felt opportunities lay everywhere, and I would not just survive but thrive.

Marcus got up, gave us a Nazi salute, and did the Hitler march. I froze. The fact that he was German and did that made the whole thing look creepy. But I said nothing. Julie sprang to her feet, joining the march. Others, including me, laughed – a brief, mirthless chuckle.

Since I was a child, I have felt lost and alone. After the sexual assault, my emotional world shut down, and I told no one about the incident, including my parents. Keeping it all to myself, I had camped in a ravine.

Strengthened by my friends, I wanted to crawl out, to feel free. But the past still weighed me down. The frail me reached for the hand that extended without questioning.

Marcus's marching was offensive, and I should have told him so. But the fear of being alienated silenced me. It would not be for many more years until I gained my voice and strength to point out wrongdoings.

Takeshi started humming a beautiful Japanese folk song. His voice was softly mellifluous.

A sense of serenity seeped through my skin, traveling into my heart. Mesmerized by Takeshi's melancholy melody, we quieted and listened.

The song faded, sweeping away some of our worries, in the way that reaching the conclusion of a Greek tragedy can make life feel less unendurable.

The air, crisp and calm, bestowed us with a delicious moment – a fugitive spot in time where we found solace.

Ricky picked up the beat. He began by cracking light jokes about his old life back in London, stealing cars to get his father's attention. Ricky spoke as though the stories belonged to others. It was as if he tried to keep himself away from that other self – the self that seemed at once intimate and alien to him. Next, he tackled an edgier issue: the similarities and differences between the English, Scottish, Welsh, and Northern Irish. It was my introduction to the United Kingdom. I realized those four kinds of British people didn't talk to each other in our hostel.

Most Hong Kong people came from Guangdong province, whereas we, the Fujianese who mostly speak Hokkien, are *ngoi saang ran* [people from other provinces], the outsiders. We learn Cantonese and try to fit in. But our accent often betrays us and attracts inquisitive or, worse, denigrating looks. I turned to Kate and smiled sadly. She put her arm around my shoulders, rocking me.

Finally, I managed to put my lonely fourteen-year-old self behind me. When needed, I had people to turn to now. The realization gave me joyous rapture, and such pleasure propelled me to stand up and walk toward the thick brick balustrade.

I took off my shoes and climbed on top of the low, wide wall. The small stones on its surface stabbed at the soles of my feet. I steadied myself and rose. Spreading my arms, I took a few baby steps forward and quivered like a fledgling. Park and Kate came over, staying close. It would be good to eliminate all the shame, guilt, and anger with one jump. But then I heard the song that begins:

Don't ask me where I come from
My hometown is far away

Why do I wander
Wander afar

The wind gusted. I swayed and cried. Kate seized my forearm; Park grabbed at my leg. Julie, Takeshi, Marcus, and Ricky came running. They reached out and held on to me.

My body recovered its equilibrium; I stood back up, taller and steadier than before. I gave my gang a grin, and they returned it with sweet smiles.

Taking a gleeful glance at the glimmering road ahead, I drew a deep breath, turned back to them, and jumped.

I landed in the outstretched arms of Park. Others joined, and we group-hugged. I felt like a lustrous, pristine pearl protected by my gang, my shell.

Later, we sat atop the short wall and looked at the harbor. I closed my eyes and imagined the dawn that would come – the sky resembling a prism with all the colors blending perfectly into each other, the sun peeking over the horizon and its brilliant rays shining brightly, the glistening reflection of the sun on the ocean. My heart swelled with awe and excitement.

Having an English name could feel advanced and Westernized, and it could also enhance communication, making it easier for international friends to pronounce and remember. Like a symbol, an English name is more memorable than the mostly double-barreled Chinese first names.

For instance, the names of the main characters in *Dream of the Red Chamber* – Baochai, Baoyu, and Daiyu – could be challenging for Western readers to remember who was who and know what their gender was.

However, I chose to have an English name because I wanted to put my past behind me. Letting go of the past and starting anew felt necessary. The English name I gave myself could reflect the new and hard-earned independent life I began leading.

Naming oneself could be empowering. It also resembled the act of breaking free – a renewal. So, I started searching for a name that embodied the merits that I admired.

Ricky highly recommended the name Sonia. He told me it was of Greek origin and meant wisdom. It immediately appealed to me because my mother's first name is Wingwai, with *Wing* meaning forever and *Wai* wisdom.

Moreover, my other friends from the mansions – Kate, Julie, and Marcus – also told me that they loved the name Sonia because it represented beauty, intelligence, and friendliness. It also resembled strength and determination. These qualities inspired me, so I became Sonia.

Then I found a job in a record shop and moved out of Chungking Mansions. I rented a sub-divided flat, also in TST, and finally had my own space to go with my new name. Keeping Fongling within me, I embarked on a new journey as Sonia.

Girls Like Us

The summer of 1994 was late, and so was Jeremy.

The bauhinia trees lining Granville Road, near Kowloon Park in Tsim Sha Tsui, were still spring trees, craggy, pocked, and misty with morning drizzle.

"Sorry, Sonia, I overslept," Jeremy called out as he ran toward me.

I stood in front of the record shop where we worked.

Out of breath, Jeremy got close, embracing me with his fresh and aquatic scent.

"It's okay. Late band practise, huh?"

He nodded and grinned.

Even in a hurry, Jeremy kept his perfect grooming – his natural curly hair plastered down, dressed in a crisp white shirt with blue jeans that fitted well on his tall and slim frame, exuding natural sophistication. But something sharp like a sword's tip beamed from his eyes, glittering and slitting through his veil of calmness.

Jeremy fished for the keys, rattled the shutters, and opened the shop.

Our store had three sections. The part from the entrance straight down belonged to Jeremy's international pop. To his left was the local portion I looked after and a counter with a cash register and a hi-fi system. The manager, Sam, took care of jazz and classical at the back, close to a tiny office.

I had joined the shop three months ago, replacing someone who Sam fired.

Jeremy had worked there for about a year. His father, a Korean businessman in Hong Kong, and his mother, a traditional Chinese housewife, expected him, their only son, to pursue higher education, preferably at Oxford or Cambridge, or join the family business.

Jeremy graduated from St. Paul's School — a top boys-only boarding school in London. He took six A-level subjects and got superb results. But when he returned to Hong Kong in the summer after the exams, he met some guys playing music in a pub and joined them instead.

"What do you fancy? Eric Clapton's *Layla,* perhaps?"

Jeremy waved the album *Unplugged* from his aisle.

Eric Clapton was Jeremy's god. The rocker's exceptional guitar-playing skills amazed Jeremy and inspired him to pick up the guitar, organize a band, and create his own music.

"It's a bit too early for it. How about this?"

I waved back with Tat Ming Pair's *The Story of the Stone.*

We opened the shop at 10:30am. Sam arrived at 11am. He would take the previous day's cash that Jeremy locked in a box inside the office and bank it, his morning ritual.

From the shop's opening to Sam's return from the bank, about an hour, was the most precious time for Jeremy and me. We could play any tracks we liked without Sam nagging us for not being more sales-oriented. He repeatedly urged us to play the current hot picks.

"If we aren't achieving our sales target, we haven't pushed hard enough. So push!" was Sam's favorite refrain.

"Good choice," Jeremy replied with a smile and added:

"Tat Ming is a unique, high-quality band. I'm glad it has become popular in Hong Kong."

"Delighted to have your approval! What do you think about this first album of the duo?"

Since I did not have a musical background, I often asked Jeremy for information about the singers, bands, and albums to better communicate with the customers.

"This album exhibits many fine qualities such as driving electronic rhythms, strong melodies, and exquisite lyrics packed with cinematic and literary allusions."

Listening to him, I felt my world was getting broader and brighter. His eyes beheld mine.

"The record concerns the people in Hong Kong's political and social margins."

It was thrilling that I understood what Jeremy said about Tat Ming's songs, which had literary lyrics. I knew the album's title – *The Story of the Stone* – was another name for *Dream of the Red Chamber*.

However, I could not comprehend the rest of the technical aspects and the writing that involved the social issues that Jeremy described. I began reading voraciously to catch up with him.

The record shop's door sang.

"Morning, guys." Sam entered and greeted us as he walked toward the office.

Jeremy and I replenished CD stocks and cleaned the racks.

The door chimed frantically.

"Don't move!"

It felt like a sharp squawk shooting through the air. I looked to the doorway.

Two men wearing black masks rushed in. One of them, the short one, locked the door behind him. Both of them stepped forward, wielding long knives. The other, medium-built, hastened toward Sam's room.

The short one pointed to me and shouted:

"Go over there and join the guy!"

He followed me as I went.

"Both of you kneel!"

Jeremy reached out for my hand and squeezed.

"Put your hands over your heads!" the short man yelled at us from behind.

Jeremy kept his eyes on mine.

The medium-built guy in the room shouted to Sam:

"Take out the cash box!"

Silence.

"Hurry up, move! Do you want to see some blood?"

Sam murmured something I could not hear.

"See, it isn't hard, is it? Open the box and empty the cash into this bag!"

Uncanny silence fell for a moment. Squeaking and hissing sounds followed.

"Well done! Go and kneel with them."

Sam knelt next to Jeremy.

The two robbers back-pedalled toward the door with their knives waving at us.

Sam and Jeremy stole a quick look at each other.

The medium-built bloke bellowed:

"Stay put! Don't move!"

The short fellow turned to the door, unlocked it, and they ran out.

Silence fell upon us like a cloud of dust after a truck roaring down a dusty road.

Gradually, Jeremy and I beheld each other as if we had just woken from a distressing dream.

He helped me up and hugged me until my shaking subsided.

We both quit our jobs on that day.

Autumn arrived.

At about 6:30pm on 20 October 1994, I ambled along Haiphong Road in TST.

Walking from Canton Road toward Nathan Road, I passed the Earth God shrine on the opposite side, which was said to be at least one hundred years old.

Joss sticks' smoke still filled the temple from dawn to dusk. The smoke would have drifted next door through all those years, stinging the eyes of the market vendors and visitors.

The rest of Haiphong Road was a jumble of post-war buildings, with their ground floors crowded with restaurants and shops for clothes, shoes, watches, and souvenirs.

I walked closer to the stone wall circling Kowloon Park. The trees' dense green foliage stretched out from the park and provided canopies over pedestrians during the scorching summertime.

Autumn was the season that best suited Hong Kong. The weather was wonderfully warm, without summer's brutal humidity and searing temperatures. The abundant sun shone mildly.

I strolled past the park's entrance. Across the gate, the bauhinia trees in full bloom adorned the slope with multiple flowers, including purple, rose, and pink. The trees' butterfly-shaped leaves billowed blithely in the breeze of dusk.

A roasted chestnut vendor stood a few steps away, holding a long turner, turning the dark coals and chestnuts-in-shells in a massive wok. Nutty fragrance permeated the air.

I dodged a few people to pass the vendor. A tall guy appeared in a crisp white shirt and walked toward me. His head was low as if he was contemplating something serious.

"Hi, Jeremy!"

I ran toward him.

"Oh, hi, Sonia! How great to see you!"

"Hope I'm not disturbing you."

"No, not at all. I was just daydreaming."

Cheeks flushed, he quickly added: "Wow, it's amazing to see you again!"

"Thanks! I'm thrilled to see you too. How have you been?"

"Long story. Shall we go for a bite to eat and chat?"

"Yes, let's."

Jeremy led me to a nearby Korean restaurant with home-style cooking that he knew I would like.

A chubby woman behind the counter, in her mid-fifties with a big head of curls, greeted us with a simple nod.

On the off-colored wall hung four outsize posters. One featured a beautiful Korean woman in *hanbok*, cradling a soju in her palms with a beatific smile.

We sat, the model's sublime smile shining above me. Her otherworldliness, like a key, unlocked something in me as I heard myself saying to Jeremy:

"Today is my twentieth birthday."

"Happy birthday!"

"Thank you."

"Let's celebrate!"

I never thought my birthday was worthy of celebration.

Jeremy signaled the woman at the counter to come over.

He called her *Imonim* ("my aged aunt") and began ordering.

"Pork Bulgogi, Soft Tofu Stew, Mixed Seafood Stew, Spicy Stir-Fried Octopus, Hotpot Mixed Rice, and..."

"Wait, only two of you, right?"

"Yes."

"You've ordered too much. No way you guys can finish it."

Stern-faced, she continued.

"You know we serve in family size, right?"

"Yes, but it's my friend's birthday. I want to celebrate with her."

"Okay, let me give you these dishes and see how it goes."

"Good suggestion," I interjected, smiling at *Imonim* and Jeremy.

"Okay then, please give us a bottle of Chamisul soju."

Imonim moved closer, lowered herself, hugged, and blessed me – a sweet surprise. Her warmth and words were what I had longed for from my mother, and which remained a longing.

When *Imonim* left, Jeremy chuckled and said:

"If she worked in our record shop, Sam would fire her for reducing customer orders!"

"Yes, indeed."

I chuckled, still feeling her arms around me.

"Do you think the guy Sam fired was behind the robbery?"

"It's possible."

Jeremy gave me a sad look; he knew the guy.

"There's another possibility. Sam refused to pay a protection fee for a month or two, claiming the business was not good. It might be a lesson given by the collectors."

He went on.

"Either way, those two robbers came fully prepared. They knew our operation too well."

"Why did Sam say so little to the police? Also, didn't we need to assist the police further?"

"Sam went to the station and canceled the case, claiming it was a misunderstanding."

Jeremy paused.

"Sam feared that whoever was behind this had a Triad background and something worse could happen to him or his family."

"It's wise for us to leave the job."

"For safety reasons, yes." He added: "But I've missed working with you. I've missed you, Sonia."

His face turned scarlet.

"I've missed you too, Jeremy. It was wonderful working with you. You taught me a lot. Thank you!"

"The pleasure was all mine!"

Looking into my eyes, he gave me an emphatic nod as if to put a seal on our friendship and something beyond. He kept his gaze on me, confirming that extra something.

My heart started singing. As if Jeremy could hear it, he beamed with delight.

But as he resumed his talk, his face dimmed.

"Since I had no job, my father persuaded me to join him. I work at his Seoul headquarters now."

A frown creased his forehead.

"My father kept telling me how hard it was for him to create his kingdom in Korea and Hong Kong, and since I am his only son, I should inherit it and expand it."

"It's nice of you to join him. Your mum must be glad. You'll excel and do them proud."

But I added:

"I'll always treasure the rocker in you."

"Thanks!" He shone.

"I wanted to invite you to my band's first show at a music festival."

His eyes lingered on my hand above the table as if a butterfly was perching on it.

"But we withdrew from it. My parents didn't want me to stay in Hong Kong any longer. They feared I would change my mind and go down another wrong track."

"That's too bad. I don't think you were on the wrong track, though!"

He needed to believe this.

"You followed your heart and pursued your dream. I haven't had the chance to watch you play and listen to your music, but I'm sure it must count for something."

I hurried to tell him how much I cared about his artistic self.

"When you told me about Eric Clapton, Pink Floyd, David Bowie, Blur, Oasis, the fire in your eyes was so palpable, beautiful."

"Thank you, Sonia!"

Our eyes reconnected, and Jeremy clung to my gaze as if to rekindle the fire I saw in him.

Dishes began filling the table.

Jeremy poured me soju and raised his glass to me.

"Happy birthday! It's so lucky of me to celebrate with you!"

My cheeks became scorching. It was the first time I ever experienced celebrating my birthday with someone so full of passion and heart.

We drank, ate, chatted, laughed, and caroused. Our glasses clinked, and the tips of our chopsticks bumped into each other repeatedly.

"Oh yes, Sonia, my uncle came with me from Seoul to visit some Guangzhou customers. He asked me to join him at *Cat* in TST East tonight. Please come with me!"

"No, but…"

"Please! My uncle is fun. I promise."

His eagerness transmitted through his pleading eyes melted away my resistance.

When we arrived later that night, his uncle was sitting at the club's best table, surrounded by his friends. The oval marble table with an arced leather sofa took up one-third of the club's upper floor.

From the seat, the whole club's view spread out: the big, open dance area in front but on a floor below, the tables on both levels, the internal spiral staircase, the bar area, and the spaces in between, all vibrating.

The uncle's friends were business people, mainly men in their forties with their female partners. But those men's eyes wandered off to the teeming dance area below, where a group of gorgeous model-like young ladies with long legs were dancing.

The clubbers were shrouded in clouds of smoke, both artificial and cigarette.

Once Jeremy's passionate uncle heard that it was my birthday, he stretched his arm out, made a big half-circle encompassing the revelers, and asked me to choose any guy or girl (he beamed at me as he said this) I liked among them. He would get me anyone I fancied.

Jeremy, nervous and embarrassed, urged his uncle to stop joking.

His uncle retorted that he meant it and suggested this or that guy to me. After a while, he sensed that Jeremy was genuinely upset and stopped. But he kept the drinks coming our way.

Jeremy and I sat at the sofa's left tip, furthest away from the throng. He seated me at the end of the couch, shielding me entirely from his uncle's sight.

At first, Jeremy sat upright with his arm along the back of the sofa behind me. Then he slid down slightly. When my body tilted toward him, he wrapped his arm around my shoulders and softly maneuvered me closer to him.

I burrowed my face into his chest, feeling his potent heartbeat. The music, conversation, and laughter roared all around. We sat still for many minutes, which flowed by us like a gurgling brook with the kisses of the sun upon it.

Suddenly, I worried that my face oil might stain his white shirt. He seemed to sense my discomfort as he searched for my eyes and questioned.

Putting his ear next to my mouth, he awaited my reply. I breathed into his ear my concern. He raised his head, regarded me for a second or two, shook his head gently, and smiled – a radiant smile.

He lowered his lips and brushed against my forehead, eyebrow, eye, cheek, lips, ear lobe, and the middle of my neck, where a scar happened to be.

I quivered but held on to him. He folded me deeper into him with one arm, and another reached my lower back, supporting me. Enclosed in his affection, I loosened, and my face nuzzled into his chest. His heartbeat thudded in sync with mine.

Eventually, the drinks got to me as my head became lighter and my eyelids heavier.

Jeremy and I left together.

I spent the night with him.

After that night, Jeremy called and called.

He left one message after another. But I ignored him.

As someone who had been the least favorite child, a sexual assault survivor, and a run-away-from-home girl, I felt utterly unworthy of love.

I would become his burden, his undoing. His parents would never forgive me.

Also, I convinced myself that Jeremy would leave me if he knew me better. And when he did, I would not know how to deal with myself again.

There would be no more broken pieces like before. It had taken me years to weave the scraps back together after my rape. The threads that held those fragments together were as tenuous as a spider's web. I couldn't invite anyone into that web. We both would fall.

These pernicious thoughts prevented me from seeing him again.

The bauhinia trees continued their glorious blooming.

I floated around like a specter.

It woke me when my period did not come almost two months later. Because my period had been regular, trepidation rained down.

One day after work, I bought a pregnancy test kit and dragged myself to a public toilet in Kowloon Park. Hiding in the most inner cell, I read and reread the instructions for the test tube. Then, I drew a deep breath and performed the test.

The control line on the left-hand side was visible, signifying that the test had worked.

I inhaled deeply. The stench of the detergent rushed to my brain, almost knocking me out.

Steadying myself with one hand pressed against the wall while the other lowered the toilet cover, I sat down. My brain blanked out.

When I again regarded the test tube, a pale purple line on the control bar's right-hand side deepened. I looked hard at it. Then I rubbed my eyes and looked again.

All sensations hit me at once – dense, salty, and fishy – like blood in my mouth.

I felt like vomiting. Shutting my eyes, I let the urge subside.

A few seconds passed. I stared at the tube, willing the line to dissipate. Instead, the violet made an indelible mark. I ditched the tester and fled.

The park existed under the cloak of dimness.

A few souls hung about. The yellowish lightbulbs sat above green poles, looking out of place and forlorn.

Even the full-bloomed Hong Kong orchid trees seemed overburdened.

I roamed the empty playground.

The kids' romping noise bawled ferociously in my head.

I escaped.

Lurching onto the trails, I found the looming banyan trees unsettling and their exposed roots stifling. I hastened out of the park's side gate.

Pacing across a bridge toward the China Hong Kong City building, I started running.

Then, I ventured onto an outdoor corridor. Hong Kong Island's skyline overwhelmed me.

I hurried through the passage and arrived at the corridor's end.

A gray and fretful harbor smashed its waves against the wall.

The wind blew hard at my face, fierce and chilly.

Such gusty winds whipped tears from my eyes.

Through a month of quiet research, I discovered the Family Planning Association of Hong Kong that would help pregnant girls like me.

I made an appointment with the FPA and went to their Wan Chai clinic. The staff members there provided me with information and counseling sessions. They accepted my booking when it was clear that I understood all the implications and consequences. The abortion would take place around Christmas, the beginning of the third month of my pregnancy.

Giving birth never entered my mind. I could not offer the child a stable home with loving parents. I made Jeremy leave by losing hope of finding me. Even if I could reach out to him again, I would not. He would take responsibility and help me to raise the child.

The problem was not him. It was me.

I could not let my baby arrive in this world and grow with a mother who was like the eye of a hurricane, empty and surrounded by strong winds and water.

A deep depression descended on me. An abyss of guilt and shame developed inside me. The void sucked down any joy I might have had for my pregnancy and made me resent myself more whenever I touched my belly.

Then and there, I decided that until I could become a healthier, stronger, and better woman adept at loving and caring for her children, I would deny myself motherhood.

I never told anyone about my pregnancy or asked any friends about abortion.

It was something I had to do alone.

On the morning of the abortion, when it was my turn, a clinic helper, *Ah-yi* [aunt], came to my bed with a wheelchair and had me sit in it.

She spread a blanket over my lap before pushing me on. In her mid-forties, *Ah-yi* shared my mother's age.

When we arrived at the operating room's door, *Ah-yi* paused and said:

"You will be fine. You are in good hands."

Her tenderness nearly unstitched me.

Fighting back my tears, I raised my head and asked:

"Do you look down on girls like us?"

Ah-yi shook her head and gave me a straight, open-hearted smile.

Her non-judgmental, unflinching response steadied me.

I entered the operating room. The shifting planes of white within it consumed me.

The brilliant white lights above the operating table. The doctor's white coat, the nurses' white uniforms and shoes. The white walls. The white ceiling. The white bed sheets. All this whiteness engulfed me.

I lost my baby and a part of me in there, forever.

After the abortion, I stayed in the clinic until night fell.

I walked to a tram stop and boarded one to Central.

It was Christmas Eve. Throngs of locals, tourists, and regular commuters jam-packed the tram. I squeezed into the middle of the lower deck and held on to a steel pole.

Ding. Ding. The ordinarily charming tram's sound combined with cheerful Christmas carols, turning into an ear-piercingly unbearable cacophony.

The crowd's odor pressed against me and joined forces with the festival's intense flavor, and the stench wrapped around me, nauseating.

I gripped the pole and forced down a surge of bile that rushed to my throat. Keeping my eyes shut, I swallowed hard to prevent myself from gagging.

My legs shook. Drops of cold sweat sprouted around my brow.

Mercifully, my stop came.

I used my last bit of energy, pushed through the throng, paid the tram fare, and got off.

After a few moments on solid ground, I regained my composure.

On leaden feet, I made my way to the outer island piers.

The closer I got to the dock, the quieter the surroundings became.

The gentle harbor wind swept away some of the city's clamor.

I raised my head to catch the blissful breeze.

My body existed in an eviscerated, hollow form. The wind ran through a crack in my skull and effortlessly rushed out of the soles of my feet.

I floated onto a half-empty ferry, heading to Mui Wo, a timeworn, bucolic town on the eastern coast of Lantau Island.

For three days, I locked myself inside a hotel room.

Lying on the coarse old carpet, I curled up in a fetal position.

I avoided food.

I avoided the mirror.

I avoided light.

I avoided the bed.

I avoided the bed sheet.

It was white.

On the morning of an early winter day two months after the abortion, I received a phone message from Sam, the record shop manager. It was the first time he had reached out since I left.

Sam told me Jeremy had said goodbye and had left for Korea for good.

It was not a surprise. Yet, a pang shot through my abdomen.

I went to work feeling dazed all morning.

When it was lunch hour, I found myself walking fast toward the Korean restaurant on Hankow Road. As soon as I pushed the restaurant's door open, I came face to face with the chubby, curly-haired *Imonim* behind the counter.

My eyes got misty. Standing still in the doorway, I kept staring at *Imonim*.

She held my gaze for a long moment. Then she stepped back, opened the drawer in front of her, took out a small, square, brown paper package, and made her way to me.

I stepped forward to meet her. She handed the bundle over to me.

"For Sonia" appeared on top of the package.

Jeremy's handwriting. Long. Elegant.

I felt my heartstrings tightened.

Trying to keep my calm, I thanked *Imonim*.

She smiled sadly, opened her arms, and drew me in.

I buried myself in her embrace.

When I could not hold back my tears any longer, I wiggled free, turned, and hastened toward the door. But I did manage to stop myself at the doorway and look back.

Imonim nodded and mouthed, "Take good care of yourself."

Hugging Jeremy's package close to my chest, I hurried away from the restaurant.

My heart hammered hard. Some bauhinia trees lined the roadside.

I stopped beneath one. The tree was still blossoming, albeit the flowers did not look as bright and vibrant as they appeared in the autumn.

The tree's big, gray, green leaves created a spreading canopy and sheltered me.

I drew a deep breath, beheld the package for a second, and opened it.

Eric Clapton's album – *Unplugged* – emerged.

I lifted the CD cover. A neatly folded letter was on the disc.

Dear Sonia:

Sorry (it seems I apologize to you a lot, or maybe not enough…,) I could not gift you a CD of my music. But as you know, this CD is my all-time favorite. I hope it can give you consolation as I have failed to do so.

I did not know what happened after that night, which stopped you from seeing me. But I must tell you: I love you very much.

My Seoul addresses and telephone numbers are on the back of this letter.

I await you. Please change your mind and open up to me once more.

Let us meet and talk. We can sort things out.

Just give me a sign or anything, and I will take the next flight
back to you immediately.

Yours with long-lasting love,
Jeremy

I refolded the letter the way Jeremy had folded it, following the
creases.

Putting it back and holding the CD close to my heart, I raised my
head.

A white cloud floated in between the tree's foliage. Another glided by.

The two clouds' edges touched, overlapped for a split second, and
started drifting apart, moving ever so slowly and farther away from each
other.

The moment of our overlapping could occur due to our yearnings for
one life toward another, full of indefinable joy, indefinite sorrow, and
everything in between.

I gathered myself and started walking away.

But at the back of my mind, these questions arose:

Could I connect, settle, and build a family and home?

Could I love and receive love naturally one day?

My feet felt heavy as the road in front seemed grim, crooked, and
endless.

Jeremy and I never met again.

He did well with his family business and moved to the UK to head up
a new branch. He picked up his guitar again and played in public from
time to time.

My menstruation stopped for two years following the abortion. When
it recommenced, it was scarce and deadly brown.

I never regretted that night.

For some reason, I kept thinking the baby would be a girl.

I would have named her Layla.

The phantom of Layla remains in me.

It becomes my menstrual pain and torments me sometimes. I accept it.

Even now, as I reach menopause, I still feel the pain.

I know Layla will live on with me until I take my last breath.

Work, Study, Family

In 1994 Hard Rock Café International launched an ambitious investment plan in Hong Kong. They leased five floors in a brand-new building at 100 Canton Road (also its name), in Tsim Sha Tsui, Kowloon.

Hard Rock made the fifth floor into its company's Hong Kong headquarters. From the ground floor to the fourth level were restaurants and bars. They also built another restaurant and bar on Swire House's ground floor in Central on Hong Kong Island side. It was one of the world's highest-priced corner shops.

The demand for staff at all levels was massive for this new company to roll out its enormous project on both sides of the harbor. Hence, they posted full-page recruitment advertisements in various local newspapers for weeks.

One day, I studied the advertisements closely and found that the cashier post did not require experience. So, I decided to apply for it.

My only work experience was as a shopkeeper, first at a gift shop inside the Star Ferry pier for a year and, subsequently, for a few months at the record shop.

I entered the lobby of 100 Canton Road and rode the lift to the fifth floor, where Hard Rock Café Hong Kong's headquarters would soon be open.

Once I arrived at the office floor, I found a vast job exhibition hall extending in front of my eyes. The interior decoration work was still in progress. Some tables and chairs lay around the enormous banquet hall-like open space.

There were signs for different departments on silver-colored stands. The person in charge sat next to each metal post. All the managers were engaged in interviews. Behind them, many applicants sat, waiting.

The candidates looked fully prepared – dressed in formal outfits, holding their diplomas, and sitting upright and poised.

On the contrary, I wore jeans and a T-shirt with my short, untamed hair.

But if I went back to get changed, I might chicken out and never return. Anyhow, I did not have presentable clothes. Instructing myself to focus on finding the financial department's signage, I pushed on.

The sign I was looking for appeared, leading me to a separate room at the far end of the hall. The door was on the right-hand side of the passage. I walked toward it, heart beating hard, wondering if the manager would take me seriously given my inappropriate outfit.

Once I reached the open door of the room, I peeked in.

In his late thirties, a medium-built, pale-skinned, frizzy-haired, Chinese-looking man sat at a grand head table before six tables divided into two lines of three. The man wore a pair of rimless, round glasses and was reading some documents.

I arrived at a good time as no one else was there with him. It saved me time queuing up. More importantly, it prevented me from sneaking away. Since I was worried sick about my looks and lack of experience, the waiting might intensify these negative thoughts and drive me out.

But I was afraid to disturb the man. So I stood by the door, willing him to sense my presence and look up to acknowledge me first.

But a few moments later, he still did not stir.

I pushed myself to knock lightly on the door.

He raised his head.

His pair of small eyes looked triangular, and his thin-lipped mouth formed a perfect "O" shape as if he was at a total loss.

Quickly, I said:

"Sorry to interrupt you, sir. I'm here for an interview."

"Fantastic. Please come in."

"Thank you, sir."

"My name is Devin Gin. I'm the Financial Controller. You can call me Devin."

His friendly manner and smile put me at ease immediately. Although I didn't know what his title meant, it sounded important.

Feeling lucky and more relaxed, I replied:

"Hi, Devin. My name is Sonia. Thank you for being willing to interview me."

"My pleasure, Sonia."

He pointed toward an empty table and the seat in front of it.

"Please sit down there and fill in the job application form."

I was relieved that he did not pay any attention to my attire; or if he did, he did not seem to mind. I went to the table and began filling in the form.

It took me less than fifteen minutes to complete.

I got up and handed it to Devin.

"So fast?"

"Yes, sorry, sir…, Devin."

I lowered my head and continued.

"I didn't have much work experience and only studied till Form 1."

"I see."

I let my head drop, thinking I should leave and stop wasting his time.

"But you speak quite fluent English, Sonia!"

"Thank you. I lived in Chungking Mansions for a year and had to learn English fast."

"How impressive! A young Chinese woman like yourself lived in Chungking Mansions for a year. Were you there with your family or friends then?"

"No, Devin, I lived alone in a travelers' hostel that year."

"Why? What happened? Please, have a seat and tell me more."

"It's a long story."

"No problem, please go ahead."

*

I sat before Devin's table and told him my story, from when I ran away from home and went to Taiwan until I returned.

He listened with his body leaning forward the entire time.

His eyes never left me.

When I finished, he said:

"You are such a young woman warrior!"

He went on.

"I'm half Chinese, and I've never heard a Chinese girl's story like yours."

He stopped for a moment and said:

"Bravo, I applaud you!"

It felt like a dream to hear his passionate praise.

The admiration in his eyes lit my heart and soul.

How unexpected – what an honor.

"Thank you so much!"

I had never expected to receive approval for my running away, let alone such high regard.

It was strange, marvelous, and frightening all at once.

Then, self-doubt got the better of me. I lowered my head.

As if he could sense my lack of confidence, Devin searched for my eyes and said:

"You should be very proud of yourself."

When I looked up again, he smiled and continued.

"Sonia, I need someone like you around me."

His tone was firm and sincere.

"You are brave, honest, and persistent."

He looked me in the eyes.

"Forget about the cashier post. You have great potential to do much more."

He proceeded.

"I will create a new position in my department in this office for you. Please give me a few days. I will contact you again soon."

This two-hour interview marked a turning point in my life. And most significantly, it helped me to put things into perspective.

First, I learned that my departure from home to Taiwan alone was courageous. Second, some people accepted and appreciated me for who I was and what I could do instead of what I wore. Third, where I came from was not important; where and how far I could go mattered. Last, Hong Kong had room for rule-breakers like me.

These new perspectives built my confidence – I was on the right track.

Two days after the interview, I received the promised call from Devin.

He congratulated me on becoming a food and beverage cost control assistant.

I told him I had no idea about this job.

He laughed and told me it was okay. He had created this position just for me and obtained his immediate boss's approval, the general manager.

Devin said he would find a suitable cost controller as my trainer. Before he recruited the controller, I could join the company first and work as the office assistant.

Joyously, I agreed and began working in his office right away.

Devin kept his word.

Once I started working in the accounts department of Hard Rock Café, Devin had someone teach me computer skills. Then, he hired Antony as the food and beverage cost controller.

Antony was a quiet man who gave me rudimentary knowledge about this particular accounts area in the hospitality industry. As I was hired directly by Devin, his boss, and joined the company earlier than he did,

Antony made it clear that as long as I got on with my tasks and performed them with no big mistakes, he would not interfere with my daily work. But it was also apparent that he would not teach me more. I learned another thing from him, though, which was office politics.

Anyhow, I performed the duties that Antony allocated to me. His hands-off attitude suited me well.

I improved my English communication skills because one of my tasks was working with other departments, such as the kitchen, restaurant, and bar operations. The staff members of these departments came from all over the world.

Working closely with the chefs and bartenders, I ensured that the portions of the dishes and cocktails adhered to their formulas. It was also my job to safeguard the ingredients they used according to the approved recipes.

Working in Hard Rock's kitchens, restaurants, and bars in TST and Central with chefs, bartenders, and front-of-house service staff members was amusing and enlightening. I also enjoyed learning about the wide range of food and beverage ingredients.

Even though my job was supervising the bar and kitchen staff and ensuring they did not cut corners or use larger quantities and more expensive ingredients that might increase the food and beverage costs, they still liked me.

For instance, before I performed the regular stocktake at the end of each month, the various section heads would appoint a team member to sort out their stocks so that I could count faster and more accurately. At the same time, these leaders always arranged for a tall and muscular guy to help me move things up and down. It was such a rewarding experience to work with and befriend international professionals.

But, an incredibly tedious task awaited me in my job, too.

Some days, I sat and checked every invoice for food, beverage, and equipment collected by the receiving department. After reviewing and confirming the invoices' accuracy and validity, I passed them on to the accounts payable for processing.

This tedious task dried me up. It felt like I was wasting my life by burying myself in numerous invoices daily.

I recalled my dreams: continuing study, entering university, and traveling.

These dreams had propelled me to return to Hong Kong and begin again.

I should not disregard them any longer.

The search for evening classes took off.

I came from a village in Fujian province to Hong Kong to join my family when I was twelve in 1986. As a Primary 6 student, I had not yet had one English lesson. A school accepted me, requiring that I restart at Primary 4. Therefore, when I ran away from home to Taiwan at 15, I had just completed my first secondary school year (Form 1).

In the 1980s and most of the 1990s, students were required to do five years of secondary school, Form 1 to Form 5, but only to then conduct two more years of study and take A-level examinations if they wished to attend university.

I, now at 20, still wanted to attend university. But it would be a long way: from Form 2 to Form 7. I would be 26 by the time I finished secondary school and could apply for university.

How daunting. I sweated at the thought of such an epic journey to university.

But I could still do it. That was most important.

Bracing myself, I searched for an evening school to join Form 2 instead of restarting from Form 1. Fortuitously, I stumbled upon the General Equivalency Diploma from the United States.

The GED consisted of four examinations: Mathematical Reasoning, Reasoning Through Language Arts, Social Studies, and Science. When an examinee passed these tests, the organization would reward the person with a certificate stating that she had American or Canadian high school-level academic skills.

The greatest thing I discovered then was that, for some reason, the School of Continuing Education, Hong Kong Baptist University (HKBU-SCE) had obtained the right to handle the GED exams in Hong Kong at that time. Furthermore, HKBU-SCE offered a three-month course to assist the test takers.

I enrolled in the program immediately.

Upon finishing the three-month course, I studied further on my own for nine more months. Still, I did not feel confident enough to take the exams.

However, I had exhausted all the study materials I received from HKBU-SCE's course, so I went to all the major public libraries in Hong Kong, trying to find more materials to study.

A Chinese saying goes, *Huang tian bu fu you xin ren*, or the heavens treasure the determined ones and would grant them their wishes if they persist to the end. After an extensive and unrelenting search, I discovered a comprehensive study guide to the GED at the City Hall Public Library in Central.

The following year, I self-studied the guidebook and did all the readings and further exercises that the book recommended. When the summer of 1995 came, I was an adequate examinee, took the tests, and passed all four subjects.

In October 1995, I obtained my GED certificate.

Eagerly, I sought an evening university that would accept my GED credentials.

Again, from HKBU-SCE, I found a joint program with Ohio University in the USA which offered a degree course in the evening at the HKBU campus.

The Ohio University Bachelor of Science degree on offer was in Communication. The Hong Kong program implemented a system allowing students to commence in any quarter of the year. I applied straight away.

After a month's wait, in November 1995, I received a letter from the Ohio University Hong Kong office at Baptist University congratulating me on being admitted to their program.

Once I learned such fabulous news, my younger self revived and I wished to bottle that moment – when reading the word "Congratulations" at the beginning of the letter.

The Chinese proverb, *the heavens reward the determined ones,* worked again.

I leaped over five years of secondary school studies and entered a university.

Taking up the university study promptly, I enrolled in the program's winter quarter – 3 January to 16 March 1996.

During the first quarter, I attended the required courses, including English – Fundamental Usage Skills and Algebra, and only managed C+ and B- respectively.

In the following spring quarter, I needed to do Freshman Composition: Writing and Rhetoric and Foundation of Human Communication. I barely survived the communication course and got a C. However, I had to withdraw from the first-year composition course because my English was insufficient – I could not complete the essay writing assignments.

Gutted, I plunged into learning English by reading.

The first novel in English that I ever read was *Gone with the Wind* by Margaret Mitchell. The other books I read and liked were *The Glass Menagerie* by Tennessee Williams, *The Age of Innocence* by Edith Wharton, and *Sherlock Holmes – The Complete Novels and Stories, Volume One and Volume Two*, by Sir Arthur Conan Doyle.

For the subjects I took, I devoured all their assigned textbooks from cover to cover, and I also read many recommended books in the syllabus to deepen my knowledge.

It was not until the fall quarter of 1998, two years later, that I dared to retake the first-year composition course and attained an acceptable B-.

Most of the Ohio University Hong Kong program classes took place at the David C. Lam Building (DLB) of the Baptist University's Shaw Campus in Kowloon Tong. Many lessons began at 6:30pm.

I only finished work at 6pm. It took over 15 minutes to walk from the Canton Road office through Haiphong Road to the TST underground railway, or MTR, station. The train journey took 20 minutes, and from the station to the campus needed at least 25 minutes of walking. Therefore, I would always be late for my class.

It made me anxious and worried all the time, fearing that I would miss critical information at the beginning of the lessons.

In my business attire – a jacket with a nice top and a skirt or a close-fitting dress and stilettos – I often ran up the lengthy, uphill, meandering pavements from the Kowloon Tong MTR station to DLB. Only by running could I make it to the classroom before 7pm, to avoid missing out on too much of the first part of the lecture.

Furthermore, I strived to take as many courses as possible to ensure I could finish the part-time degree program in four years as if I were doing the full-time program.

Hence, I attended classes five nights and Saturday afternoons every week. And I managed to keep this substantial schedule up for each quarter that followed.

I also participated in all four quarters, which meant for two and a half months, I would attend five nights and an afternoon, followed by a half-month break. Then, another cycle of this intense schedule repeated itself.

I worked and studied this way from January 1996 to December 1999 and only missed two classes. One was for an important evening event that I could not avoid attending, and another was for my birthday.

A friend knew I loved dance performances, so she bought two top-tier tickets to a show at the Lyric Theatre of The Hong Kong Academy for Performing Arts two months before the show for one of my birthdays. She showed me the valuable tickets and urged me to skip a class for one night and enjoy the show.

I appreciated my friend, and I wanted to go.

However, I was worried sick that I would miss out on a chapter which might affect my understanding of the following chapters.

I forgot that I had close classmates. A few of us were adult students and took our studies seriously. We made immense efforts to attend our classes. These difficulties strengthened the bonds between us. Usually, I shared my notes with them as I was the one who most likely achieved the highest attendance.

Once I told my classmates about my fear of being behind the course due to my absence, they all offered to help me and lend me their notes. Reassured, I allowed myself to skip a class and watch the show with my friend.

And again, art transformed me.

The dance show that I luxuriated in was Stomp.

Originating from Brighton, England, Stomp was a percussion group with performers who used their bodies and ordinary objects to create a physical theater performance using rhythm, acrobatics, and pantomime.

I admired Luke Cresswell and Steve McNicholas, the founders of Stomp.

They believed rhythm was the music of life.

They heard rhythm in everything, such as people running up and down steps and flicking a newspaper when they read it.

They sought rhythm from anywhere and everywhere.

Stomp opened my mind and encouraged me to recognize the rhythms of my life.

Furthermore, Stomp challenged me to hear rhythms in the sounds of everyday life.

For example, in the MTR, when I heard a train passing, I recognized the sound it made had a certain rhythm.

And in the evening school, the professors' speech and the low, slightly squeaky noise they made while writing on the boards carried an exclusive tempo. The sound of summer rain splashing against our classroom windows possessed unique beats.

Whatever I heard around me, Stomp inspired me to set my imagination free, hearing the world in new ways. It deepened my connection with my inner self and the outer universe.

The founders of Stomp drummed this into my head: When you had a passion – as they did with rhythm – daring to work hard on it, developing it into something singularly your own, your art or act might make a difference. You might make a difference.

Summer 1996 bustled by in full force. With the steady income from Hard Rock Café I felt more settled. During my time at Chungking Mansions, I visited my family's Diamond Hill home and found it empty. A neighbor told me that they had moved to an apartment in Ngau Tau Kok and told me that they still had the same telephone number. When I phoned at around 4pm on a weekday, my younger sister answered. We cried. I told her that I was not ready to go home, but I asked her to tell our parents that I had returned to Hong Kong and that I was safe.

When I finally reached out to my mother, she kept calm and told me to come home for lunch one Saturday when my father was at work. A few months later, when she felt Father had accepted the fact of my return and was mentally prepared to see me, she told me and I went home for dinner on a Sunday night. We did our best to have an uneventful meal.

I gained confidence and broadened my horizons by immersing myself in evening university studies.

It was time to find a more suitable job and move my life forward.

I would not learn more from Antony, my immediate manager; more importantly, having a career in the accounts department was not my aspiration.

After two years of working at Hard Rock, I earned a sufficient monthly salary: about $7,500. Fresh university graduates mainly got about $6,000 then.

With that salary, half went to rental and a quarter to study.

So, I had to find a job that would pay at least the same. However, it was hard because Hong Kong companies did not recognize the GED.

The office job's minimum academic qualification requirement was Form 5, secondary or high school graduation.

One day, in a newspaper's recruitment section, a small advertisement from a trading company for a marketing executive position caught my attention. The company name looked familiar. I checked and found that it was one of the suppliers to Hard Rock Café.

I rang up that trading company and asked for the person in charge of recruitment. The receptionist forwarded the line to someone who was not a native Cantonese speaker. Hence, I switched to English.

Johnny Ha introduced himself – a Malaysian Chinese and the company's managing director. He invited me over for an interview.

During the interview, I told Johnny about the Malaysian-Chinese students I met at National Taiwan University. Without them, I would not have had the action-packed and much-loved two-year journey in Taiwan.

In his early fifties, Johnny understood how hard it was to travel to another place and make a life for himself.

We clicked.

He did not ask about my qualifications. Instead, Johnny shook my hand enthusiastically before the meeting ended and welcomed me on board.

Johnny's company was a packaging supply firm. The company sold cling-wrap film and aluminum foil for industrial use in hotel and restaurant kitchens. The firm's office and production plant were in a factory building in Sha Tin, in the New Territories of Hong Kong.

They had two large machines that divided the cling-film and aluminum foil from large wheels to smaller, individual, professional kitchen sizes.

The new lighter rolls would have a long, rectangular container with a sharp blade.

As the company tried to compete with famous American brands such as Reynolds, their prior director, Johnny's partner, used a price-cutting strategy. But once Johnny took charge of the business, he implemented different policies.

Johnny taught me the most crucial lesson in marketing: Get close to the end user.

In our case, it was the chefs.

He reckoned that we should approach and befriend the chefs using the product. If they were unhappy with it, they would not use it, no matter what price the supplier offered to their purchasing department.

Therefore, my journey of dealing with chefs from the major hotels, clubs, airline catering, and restaurant chains in Hong Kong began with Johnny in mid-1996.

Soon, the work in this packaging firm became tedious and uninspiring. After all, the company only handled two dull products.

The act of penetrating the professional kitchen setting and getting to grips with dealing with the chefs, on the other hand, was incredibly intriguing. And more fascinatingly, by visiting the chefs in their kitchens, I encountered some of the finest food ingredients that the luxury hotel chefs used from all over the world. These gourmet encounters opened my eyes wide.

Soon, I was engrossed in delicate, aromatic, seductive global gastronomy.

My hunger to learn about these captivating and infinite ingredients worldwide and the desire to be part of such a culinary world was rocket-fueled.

Out of pure luck, I had befriended the executive chef of the Sheraton Hotel back then. The chef knew the managing director of a French fine foods company very well and heard that the MD was looking for someone to replace the current unsatisfactory sales manager.

The chef told me that the MD wished to recruit a local person who was assertive, resourceful, and a capable English communicator. He reckoned that I made a perfect candidate and highly recommended me to the MD.

I contacted the MD, who invited me for a lunch interview.

Somehow, I must have answered the MD's questions quite well over the short lunch meeting, for he immediately offered me the job before we parted that day.

At the beginning of 1997, I entered the fine foods supply industry in Hong Kong.

On Monday, 30 June 1997, in the afternoon, the last governor of British Hong Kong, Chris Patten, left Government House with his family for the last time.

On a TV broadcast, I saw Governor Patten come out of the house into a drizzle and leave through an honor guard of police. He stepped onto a dais, accepted a salute, and received the lowered folded Union Flag.

HMY Britannia, an elegant old ship, was moored at Tamar, awaiting the Patten family and the Prince of Wales to embark and depart.

It was there at Tamar that the British departure ceremony took place. Under thousands of umbrellas, crowds gathered for the farewell.

The rain got heavier, tipping down harder and harder.

"For Hong Kong as a whole, today is cause for celebration, not sorrow," the governor began his speech, and closed with: "Now Hong Kong people are to run Hong Kong. That is the promise, and that is the unshakable destiny."

The rain was pelting down, monsoon style.

The British flag came down, and the British administrative responsibilities met their end.

The heavens started exploding with a grand firework display.

Then, I watched the handover ceremony in the brand-new Hong Kong Convention and Exhibition Centre in Wan Chai.

The clock struck midnight and marked the transfer of the administration of Hong Kong from the United Kingdom of Great Britain and Northern Ireland to the People's Republic of China.

A new flag of Hong Kong appeared – a red field with a white, five-petalled Bauhinia flower in the center.

Enshrined in the Basic Law were the fundamental policies of China's rule over Hong Kong after the handover.

Hong Kong had a new name: the Hong Kong Special Administrative Region or HKSAR.

I had a new job: Assistant Sales Manager.

My career was on an upward trajectory.

Could the fate of the HKSAR be the same?

Many people had doubts.

Being green and eager to build my life, I could not worry about Hong Kong's future then. To me, the HKSAR was still the Promised Land.

The Joint Declaration and the Basic Law stipulated that Hong Kong would follow the "one country, two systems" principle.

The principle decreed that mainland Chinese socialism would not apply to Hong Kong. Instead, this particular region would continue its capitalist system and way of life for at least 50 years after 1997.

"Fifty years" to the 23-year-old me sounded like forever.

The HKSAR began implementing a new set of laws under a new higher power, and I commenced performing a new job under a new company in the same year.

I worked with the French fine food firm's MD from early 1997 to late 1999.

In Hong Kong, men dominated this industry. Because most chefs were men, they valued the male salespeople more highly and perceived them as more authoritative and knowledgeable.

By contrast, salesladies were there to charm and entertain the chefs. But I contributed to the lessening of such a myth. In those three years, I triumphantly built up my reputation as a professional fine food saleslady and stood tall among those salesmen.

The MD was a middle-aged, stout, and rigid Frenchman.

He ruled his firm like Mao ruled China. It was his way or no way.

The MD ran the company by absolutely adopting a patriarchal code of conduct – men were there to lead while women were there to assist.

This practice seemed to be the case with Frenchmen's management style in Hong Kong. Another Frenchman that I worked for years later, and the French managers he hired, displayed precisely the same patronizing behavior toward locals, especially when it concerned their female staff members.

I witnessed this phenomenon – French white male supremacy – in Japan and Taiwan. Later in my life, I encountered many other female business associates from the Philippines, Thailand, Vietnam, Singapore, and Mainland China who told me about this issue in these places throughout Asia.

The office of the French fine food firm that I worked for then was arranged in an L shape.

Two tables and a pantry awaited you when you walked through the main entrance. Then you turned left, and there were three rooms inside with four tables on the outside. A corridor separated them.

The first room belonged to the local male financial controller, an old subordinate of the MD from a previous company. The next one had been used by the head of sales, a man. The biggest inner room was the MD's office. Female employees, including the MD's secretary, two customer service officers, an accounts clerk, and a shipping supervisor, sat at the outside tables.

I joined the company as assistant sales manager, albeit replacing the head of sales. But instead of inheriting the guy's room, I had to sit behind the shipping supervisor. The table was the closest to the entrance, resembling a junior employment level.

I worked directly under the MD and was responsible for the company's sales development. And I outperformed the previous guy as I attained the sales targets the MD set for me every month while the salesman had not.

But, even with consistently excellent performance, the MD never offered me the same sales manager title. He kept the manager's room empty and out of my reach.

However, his hand would always find some way to reach my thigh.

Every Saturday morning, we would have a sales meeting in his office.

The MD had a large mahogany working table facing the door, a bulky, big, fine leather chair behind the table, and two blue, coarse, low office chairs in front. Next to these was a small round table with chairs in the corner.

He held the meetings with me at the corner table.

The MD would always sit in the chair closest to the wall, farthest away from the view of his secretary and another female worker outside his office. I sat on his right side.

As the meeting progressed, he would move his chair inch by inch toward me until the two chairs' edges pressed each other tightly.

He had two cups of coffee every morning, which his secretary made to perfection. Otherwise, he might have a tantrum.

His coffee breath, hot and sour, blew right into my face.

He held the printed sales report pages, and their upper edges would brush my breast from time to time.

And then, his right hand would find its way and land on my left thigh.

Everything looked accidental, casual.

And then, the MD would bring me to lunch sometimes. Those lunches usually happened after we finished the meetings with the chefs.

To show respect to his favorite few chefs, or when some restaurants or hotels were doing promotions with our products, he would dine there.

Those lunches usually turned out long and luxurious.

The chefs would put extra care into preparing for us. I enjoyed the dishes and relished one or two glasses of fine wine the MD selected for us. But his invariable physical advances toward me after those lunches were hard to stomach.

He would sometimes advance by walking me into a corner in the lift lobby and pressing his mouth against mine to steal a quick kiss.

When he had a glass too many to drink, he became even more presumptuous as he led me into some back staircases, shielded me from the view of the passers-by with his bulky body, shoved his tongue into my mouth, and his hands roamed around.

Those sexual advances occurred frequently during my first year working with the French MD.

He told me repeatedly that I was inexperienced at my job. He had bestowed the position upon me and granted me lots of his time and attention, so I should be highly grateful to him, take everything in, and keep quiet.

And that was what I did, not breathing a word to anyone else.

The MD had successfully preyed on my sense of insecurity and inferiority.

I could not hold my head high or speak loudly during his presence.

He was right. I was not good enough and never would be.

I should stop thinking and forget everything.

But I refused to give up on myself. I worked hard and learned hard.

In the almost three years I worked for the guy, I studied as many materials as possible about all kinds of fine food ingredients from France and other European countries. Then, I got them into the Hong Kong food service industry.

I explored and acquired the background stories of different kinds of ingredients, producers, distinctive features, usages, seasonal aspects, and so on.

Also, I ensured that I prepared well for my meetings with the customers and never wasted their time. Moreover, I always attempted to deliver what I had promised my customers and informed them honestly in advance on the rare occasions when I could not provide them with the goods on time.

After a while, many chefs, procurement managers, and even GMs of reputable hotels and sizable restaurant chains found me knowledgeable, helpful, efficient, and reliable. They preferred to work with me than with the MD.

Hence, I established my name in the fine food supply industry of Hong Kong.

But I was keen to speed up my progress, and I decided to quit my job in order to go to the USA to complete my degree as quickly as possible via full-time study.

Part Six: Renewal

Hong Kong & USA

1999 – 2000

Pre-USA

It would take over a year for the Ohio University program in Hong Kong to gather enough students to open the courses that remained for me to complete my degree because only a few made it to the end, and I did not want to wait that long.

I was eager to get this done. Eager to evolve.

The degree would add little to my job. I knew I could climb the corporate ladder in the food supply industry or build my own business empire if I really wished and worked hard for it.

But pursuing higher education was one of my dreams. I wanted to become a *zhi shi fen zi*, or intellectual, like my parents used to be in China.

I had resigned, hoping to attend the final four courses at Ohio University in the spring semester of 2000.

But when I applied for a student visa at the United States Consulate-General in Hong Kong, I discovered that my savings were insufficient. A requirement stated that I must have a substantial deposit in my Hong Kong bank account to prove I could support my life in the USA without trying to work there.

For the first time after I left home, I turned to my mother for help.

I knew I could repay my mother once I came back.

I asked my mother if she could lend me the money. I explained in detail that I only needed her loan to make up the US-government-required amount. I must reach a specific figure in my bank statement for them to accept my visa application.

I had met the sales targets at the French firm I had worked for over the last three years, earning good commissions on top of my salary and saving a fair amount. So I had enough for studying and living fees. I clarified all this to my mother and stressed that I would not need to use her money. I would return the total amount to her as soon as I came back.

My mother said she did not have the money. I found this very surprising because, besides my father, all of us, her four children, gave her a small portion of our monthly income. We took our filial duty seriously. I began my contribution when I started working at the Hard Rock Café. I had visited the family regularly since then. Mine was insignificant, but my elder siblings had worked for a while and probably contributed more.

Therefore, Mother should have had some savings by then.

But she shut the door firmly like a slap across my face.

She asked me to borrow from my brother and my new sister-in-law instead. They had recently married and had received quite a large sum of wedding gift money.

I did not feel close to my brother and sister-in-law and was highly reluctant to ask them for help. However, I did not have a job and could not get a bank loan.

Without any better options, I asked them eventually.

My brother and his wife told me they lent me the money out of respect for our mother.

But years later, when my sister-in-law had a glass too many to drink, she told me the money was my mother's.

My sister-in-law disclosed further that my mother had been afraid I would not return the money, so she made up the story with them to ensure that I would. Mother figured I would not dare refuse to pay them back because I was not close to my brother, and especially not to the new sister-in-law.

My mother's smiling, concerned face when she listened to my hard work and study narratives, and later, her supportive words and gestures regarding my further American study plan were all just acts.

The realization of her pretense pained me more than when I burnt the flesh around my wrist with a well-lit cigarette before running away from home.

The fact that she did not understand me and could not see the real me was shocking. She still thought so lowly and so little of me. It felt like the old wounds on my wrists, and my heart was savagely ripped open.

I fully grasped then that I had no home to return to.

I would remain a passer-by to my family for the rest of my life.

And if I could accept that, I could stop hoping and getting hurt again.

Since I ran away from home at 15, until 1999 when I was 25, my parents and three siblings moved three times. After they moved away from Diamond Hill before the government demolished the "squatter village" for good, they rented an apartment in Ngau Tau Kok because by then, Elder Sister and Elder Brother had started working and could help pay the rent. Younger Sister studied at Hong Kong University and received some grants.

Mother had surgery and retired afterward. Father and the two elder siblings could support the family in a better place with a relatively high rent. Some years later, Elder Sister got married and moved out. Luckily, my parents finally received the government settlement notice for their hut in the slum; they could live in a temporary housing area in Tai Wai in the New Territories. About two years later, they got the final settlement and moved into a housing estate in Ma On Shan.

A few years later again, Elder Brother got married and moved out, and Younger Sister began working and moved out. Now my parents had the flat to themselves.

The night before leaving for the USA, I had dinner with my parents at their place. Over the meal, I talked with Mother about the trip and my study plan, pouring out my heart to her.

I hoped Mother (and Father) would understand how seriously I took this trip, how seriously I took study, and, by extension, how seriously I took life. Initially, my father did not know I had borrowed money from the family. When he learned this, it heated the latent rage inside the volcano of his head.

Father had been drinking since the beginning of the meal, first Tsingtao beer, then *Kaoliang* [sorghum liquor], followed by Chivas Regal Scotch whisky. He drank alone and remained silent, nibbling on some food from time to time.

Suddenly, he stood up and raised his side of the table. All the dishes, cans, and bottles went smashing to the floor.

The harsh, grating sound of the porcelain bowls, plates, and glass bottles hitting the ground shook the living room.

He began to shout at me:

"You are a whore! You are a liar! You are good for nothing!"

He kept yelling and pointing at me:

"All you want to do is snatch money from us and run away!"

His roars continued:

"Study? Study my ass! Look at yourself. You are useless!"

And:

"How can you be a university student, not in a million years!"

And:

"Do you even know how to write the word 'shame'?"

His face came within an inch of mine.

"You brought on so much shame to me. I couldn't face our relatives!"

Adding:

"Not to mention the ancestors!"

He shouted even louder:

"Shame on you!"

He pointed his second finger right at my nose.

The disgust in his eyes gobbled down both of us.

The alcohol inflamed his face and infused his breath.

The density of his breath could have set the house on fire.

Like molten rocks, his rage erupted, threatening to bury me alive.

But I kept my head high and stoically fought back my tears.

There is no way I would let myself shed a tear before him.

I turned, moved toward the door, opened it, and walked out.

Like a walking corpse, I reached the lift lobby and pressed the lift button.

Some iron bars formed a railing between two lifts. I went to lean on them.

Then I looked over the fence. The ground level's gray cement floor 43 floors below was clearly in view.

Since my body was nimble, it would be easy for me to climb over the railing and jump off.

That way, Father's tormenting screams in my head could cease to exist once and for all.

"Ling, wait!"

Mother called as I heard her come running.

The lift arrived at that moment.

I reached the lift's door when Mother appeared.

"Ling, good girl, never mind your father."

She drew a deep breath and continued.

"You know your father; he has an abnormal mind and can't take any news well."

I gave Mother a nod to thank her.

Then I entered the lift.

The doors were shutting.

The lift started to descend.

My body felt so heavy I fell to the floor.

The word "whore" stuck in my mind.

It reminded me of that "Xiao Mei" incident.

I could have been a whore – a shameless girl who started selling her body at 15.

It could have been how I supported myself through those years on the road.

It was natural for Father to think that.

I knew my aunts and uncles thought that too.

I made him lose face.

He could not raise his head before them, especially whenever I was around.

Suddenly, I realized it had been five years since I started visiting home regularly. The tension – the latent rage – built up over these years in his volcano head had erupted for him.

I knew he must have been worried sick after I ran away from home.

I knew he went to the police station regularly to ask for updates.

I knew it must have been extremely tough for him. He was a very proud man, after all.

Still, I was furious with myself for trying so hard to rationalize his behavior, legitimize his verbal abuse, and normalize his insults.

No, I could not let him push me down again like he did when I was little, thinking I was the bad mud that would not stick on the wall.

I refused to think that I was a whore. I was not. I did not do it. I fought my way out, literally.

And over the five years since I returned I had been trying to tell him by telling my mother in front of him. He did not give me one chance at all. He did not open himself even slightly to other possibilities.

He condemned me.

It all came back to me.

Whenever I approached my father and asked if we could talk, he would fix his eyes on the TV and tell me to speak to my mother instead.

Unfortunately, thoughts of my mother were not soothing. She had been acting as the good one.

She often went out of her way to be nice to me and tried to prevent our relatives from gossiping about having a daughter who ran away and never returned.

I appreciated her efforts and continued to visit home and attend gatherings, especially during the large Chinese festivals. I knew maintaining a complete home for others to see had been her primary concern since the day she decided to marry my father. Therefore, I strived to carry out my part and make her proud.

But I felt the pain every time I recalled her trying, sometimes almost pleading, as she had done before the lift door closed. She could never behave naturally with me as she did with my elder brother and younger sister. With them, she was comfortable and affectionate.

When Mother was with Elder Brother or Younger Sister, her body relaxed as she put the sole of one foot over the other, leaned against the kitchen counter, and chatted away merrily. It was as if the umbilical cord between her and those two siblings remained intact.

Whenever I encountered those occasions when the three of them existed in their exclusive realm, a sense of loneliness would wash over me. I came face to face with the following facts.

I could never fit in and would never be part of them.

I did not belong to this place called home.

I needed to accept it.

My mind did, eventually.

But my heart lingered.

It refused to relent.

Because relenting meant that I let myself revert back to the young Fongling, feeling unworthy of love.

OU

I arrived at the Ohio University campus in Athens, Ohio in early March 2000.

For the first week, I stayed at the OU Inn inside the campus.

On the first day after arriving, I decided to go to the international student center to get registered. The inn's clerk looked friendly enough, so I went to him and asked for directions to the center.

He told me that I could walk there. Taking out a campus map, he showed me the way in detail and told me to keep the map.

I thanked him and got on my way.

The sky was bleak. Some dense gray clouds continued gathering in volume.

It was as if the heavy rains were ready to pour down on me at any minute.

As I did not bring an umbrella, I quickened my pace and tightened the belt on my black leather jacket, pulling it closer and letting myself feel warmer and more protected.

Reaching the top of a steep slope, I paused and looked back.

Stunning views revealed themselves in front of me. Beautiful colonial Georgian buildings, two stories high, symmetrically patterned, red-brick-walled, multi-pane windowed, stood steadfast with a chimney on each side.

A river meandered around the edges of the town as if guarding it solemnly.

The houses caught my attention as they reminded me of the ones on TV or in magazines. Seeing them in a tangible form could not be more enchanting.

Then, the river.

Its ripples might sound like a sleeping baby's heartbeat.

Soon, in my mind, the river transformed the landscape into a fairyland.

Fairies could fly out from the gorgeous Georgian houses' windows.

And when they did, they would hover over the river, fluttering their wings.

They flew on, dancing with the breeze, whispering something to each other.

The fairies released strings of tinkling laughter and charmed the fairyland further.

Being enthralled atop that steep slope, I slipped into reverie.

Thoughts about Xu Zhimo, one of the most legendary and loved romantic poets of 20th-century Chinese literature, emerged.

Xu's poem *Chance* made me raise my head and behold the clouds.

> I am a cloud in the sky
> A chance shadow on the wave of your heart
> Don't be surprised
> Or overjoyed
> In an instant, I will vanish without a trace.
> (My translation)

Reciting this first stanza of *Chance* soundlessly, I wondered if I was a "chance shadow" in the heart of this OU campus fairyland.

Even so, I did not mind as I cherished this chance to be here.

A sense of relief rushed over me, making me feel free and fabulous.

When I regarded the river again, the view awakened the memory of Xu's other poem: *Bidding Farewell to Cambridge Again.*

To seek a dream? Go punting with a long pole
Trace upstream to where the green grass is greener
With the punt that is full of starlight
And to sing out loud in its radiance.
(My translation)

Chanting this stanza from the latter half of the poem in my head, I suddenly heard a new message it was telling me, as follows.

I had evolved from the frightened 15-year-old who was once a lost ant to this competent dream-seeker today. Equipped with my "long pole," my determination, I would go far.

Starlight refilled the room in my chest, allowing me "to sing out loud in its radiance."

The semester would start in one week.

A quiescent mood shrouded the campus.

Such a gentle, calm atmosphere increased its magical spell on me.

The campus drew me closer to her breast, offering me time to rest.

To renew.

It felt like home here.

I decided to move into the campus.

The administration office assigned me to the East Green residence hall.

My dormitory was in the oldest and most traditional hall on campus.

More importantly, it was in one of those fairy houses that I adored.

When I first went to find my dormitory, the trees on both sides of the road had small leafy branches coming out.

The new twigs looked fragile yet full of vitality.

They seemed so eager to grow thick and strong.

Shy sunbeams seeped through these novel, delicate branches.

The sunlight was warm and gentle.

I found the dormitory room at East Green.

After giving its door a light knock, I asked:

"Can I come in?"

"Yes," a young woman's voice answered me.

When I pushed the door open and stepped inside, an American girl greeted me.

She was short and chubby. It seemed the baby fat was still clinging to her.

"Hi! I'm Tara."

She smiled sweetly.

"Oh, hi Tara, I'm Sonia. Nice to meet you."

Her youth and bubbliness reminded me that I was a mature student.

For a moment, I felt self-conscious.

"Nice to meet you too, Sonia. You must be our new roommate. Welcome!"

"Yes, thanks!"

Tara's laid-back air calmed me. She reduced my fear of being singled out and feeling awkward.

Tara pointed to an empty bunk bed and said I could choose the upper or lower one as I wished because we only had three students here this semester. She also mentioned that a study table, chair, and closet next to the bed belonged to me.

I thanked her and sat down on the lower bed.

The whole setup was simple and easy, just the way I liked it.

My area inside the room was on the right-hand side of the door.

A nice, old-fashioned large window was in the middle, with our desks facing it.

Tara and another girl named Sandy, whom I met later, shared the left side's bunk bed. The two came from Cleveland and had been best friends since high school.

Sandy turned out to be the antithesis of Tara in every aspect. She was tall, slim, timid, and seldom spoke or smiled. Her fair skin gave rise to blushes and freckles.

Sandy remained polite and distant.

We nodded to each other once or twice a day, acknowledging each other's existence.

My first culture shock came from the ladies' shower room.

There were two shower rooms on each floor, one for boys and one for girls.

The girls' shower room was close to our room. I used to go in there fully dressed. After showering and drying, I dressed again and returned to our room.

Some Western girls walked freely inside the shower room, only wrapping themselves in a bath towel, sometimes even without it.

I had hardly looked at my own naked body, let alone had others see it.

I disliked my body then. Also, I was both competitive and insecure as I often noticed other girls' fine features and felt inferior.

Over time, it became apparent that it was the confident young women who would wrap their bath towels in the shower room, especially those who wrapped them low around their breasts and tucked the end into their cleavage, and those who went naked. These girls often took time to shave their legs or dry their hair. They were not necessarily the ones in great shape.

For instance, Tara walked around comfortably in her bath towel, but not Sandy.

In the boys' presence, some girls wrapped in bath towels lingered in the corridor.

The boys pretended not to pay much attention to these girls in towels, but we all knew they did. It was like watching a cat-and-mouse game.

I was glad to see the young women comfortable in their skin. At the same time, I felt slightly sad as some did not treasure their bodies well.

But I did not cherish my body well either. I had let that French MD touch and kiss me against my will.

I was intimidated and dared not to make the slightest movement during those times, fearing it would appear as a sign of protest.

For the tiniest sign of protest would unveil the ugliness of his behavior. It would cause him embarrassment and cost me my job.

Sensing my vulnerability, the French MD had taken full advantage.

He made me an object.

I was not a person to him in those moments when he launched his sexual advances.

I was, at best, an easy target, a pleasing thing, a conquerable body.

Deep down, I knew there lay the core reason why I could not get the courage to say:

Please stop.

The main reason was I felt powerless.

As if Coach's assault had only happened yesterday, I vividly recalled the following:

What it felt like to have my body pinned to a bed.

To have the hem of my school dress pushed up.

To have my legs forced apart.

To be penetrated.

It made no difference to say:

Please stop.

It became evident that my emotional self had not been growing with the intellectual self I had developed through my intensive studies.

Also, I finally dared admit to myself that the ultimate factor that made me resign from the sales job, fight so hard to obtain the funds and get the visa approved, and fly so far away from that French MD, from the industry, from my family, was that:

My emotional self was severely in need of nurturing.

I felt the pain.

Like a wounded animal that would go into the woods, find a quiet place, and stay without moving for days, I needed to find myself that safe spot.

The spring semester began.

As a student majoring in Communication, I needed to take four final courses to obtain my degree. The lectures included Communication and Interpersonal Relationships, Practices in Organizational Communication, Communication and Persuasion, and Meeting and Conference Planning.

Eagerly, I attended these classes at Scripps College of Communication on Union Street on the OU campus.

Ohio University prides itself on being a culturally diverse campus. However, I only met one or two Asian students in each of the four classes that I took when each class's size was about 40 students on average. I found the professors were informal and friendly which led to my second, and helpful, cultural shock.

Hong Kong had been under British administration until very recently, and we followed the English way of addressing people appropriately. It coincided with our Chinese culture, and I was glad to follow it. Thus, for university professors, we would address them respectfully as Dr. So-and-so.

One of my professors on the OU campus was Dr. Roger Aden.

In his early fifties, he was medium built, scholarly, wise-looking with oval-shaped glasses, and nearly bald.

I addressed him as Dr. Aden when I attended his first class. As I was sitting at the back, some students turned around and gave me funny looks.

Dr. Aden used the situation and took the time to introduce the cultural and historical background of Hong Kong to the mostly American students in our class. He asked them to respect the differences and the diversity of our world.

Then he turned to me, looked me straight in the eye, and told me in an amiable tone that I could call him Roger.

It had been unthinkable to me to address a senior person, let alone a professor, by their first name. But Dr. Aden's warm and open style put everyone, including me, at ease.

I looked at him and nodded – acknowledging my comprehension of his words and showing appreciation for his kindness in including me.

He winked and smiled back.

This seemingly minor incident had a significant impact on me.

It made me feel respected.

Also, it added gravity to my presence.

A new sense of self-respect began to grow.

And the growth enhanced my confidence.

The new self-confidence, in turn, cultivated self-acceptance.

My self-esteem started repairing itself.

And I could permit myself to think that:

Yes, it was okay to be me, and it was okay for me to be different.

I became more self-assured and willing to speak out more frequently in Roger's class and the rest of the lessons I attended.

Roger was about my father's age. Unfortunately, he also brought back some unpleasant memories I had about my father.

When my father realized I had run away from home when I was 15, he returned to his hometown and cried in front of his ancestors' gravestones for having a disgraceful daughter like me.

I heard the story about my father crying over the dishonorable me from my mother and other relatives. After that, I began to see the following graphic scene in my mind's eye over and over again.

Like watching a movie, the story started in an idyllic valley of our hometown in Nan'an, Fujian, China.

Tie Guan Yin, Iron Buddha tea, its nutty, honeyed, orchid fragrance shrouded the valley. Such tea plants grew in the terraced fields of the surrounding hills. A light breeze of an early winter afternoon blew.

Velvety tea tree sprouts sang in a softly mellifluous voice, announcing their arrival and readiness to be picked and made into the finest *Tie Guan Yin,* a premium variety of the oolong tea in 19th-century Fujian.

Suddenly, a piercing cry shattered the serenity of the valley.

"I wish I were dead rather than having a daughter like that!"

My father collapsed onto the cement floor in the middle of his ancestors' graveyard.

His grandparents' and parents' tombstones encircled the graveyard within the valley of his hometown.

His head dropped. His body slumped.

His rage, despair, shame, guilt, and regret churned inside him.

Those hateful words he shouted out earlier were flaming arrows, and they shot through the hearts of the people nearby.

My mother stood behind my father solemnly. Her hands were folded. She held them tightly in front of her cross-shoulder handbag, pressing it down forcefully.

But the look on her face spoke indifference in volumes. It was as if she was very used to her husband's nervous breakdown.

His emotional uproar and outlandish cries had long lost their effect on her.

She had made up her mind to be unmoved and unaffected by his behavior, however ridiculous it was. Thus, there was no sign of her reaching out to her husband.

Instead, with her body slightly arched, she stayed a step away from him.

If cold looks could put out the fires burning in my father's soul, the coldness in my mother's eyes would complete the job fast and effectively.

Uninterrupted, Father's tears rushed down his cheeks. Tears rolled down his nose and mixed with phlegm. They dripped down from his chin to the ground.

My fifth uncle stepped forward. He tried to pull my father up.

But Father refused. He screamed and became more hysterical.

He brushed away Fifth Uncle's hand and plunged to the ground.

My other uncles were all present as well. They stood somberly close like my mother, forming a crescent moon shape behind my father.

The third and sixth uncles put their hands behind their backs.

The fourth and seventh uncles placed theirs rigidly by their sides and forced their backs to straighten up.

The uncles' first and middle fingers had brown-yellowish stains on the sides of the fingertips. The fingers were jerking momentarily.

It was a sign of dying from cigarettes as they were heavy smokers. But none of them dared leave or make a sound that might attract unnecessary attention to themselves at that moment.

A gust of wind came dashing and brought along the *Tie Guan Yin*'s refreshing scent.

But then, burning straw stubble, which an action to prepare for the coming spring plowing, had a robust odor as the burning happened in a harvested, soggy rice paddy field next to the graveyard.

This pungent stench swallowed the subtle, pleasant scent of the tea plants.

The smoldering of the unsuccessful stubble burning created a thick layer of smoke, choking everyone there. The uncles covered their mouths and coughed quietly.

Father's voice was still the dominant one.

His sobbing sounds synchronized with the background hum of the smoldering straw roots.

And then together the two somehow created a soothing symphony reverberating in the valley.

The reverberation calmed the scene.

Father wore his usual gray windbreaker, a white undershirt, a bleached shirt with alternating broad and narrow light blue stripes, and black trousers.

The square frames of his thick glasses were midnight dark.

They pressed down heavily, the two supporting points of the glasses making permanent dents on either side of the bridge of his nose even when he removed them, which he did then.

The afternoon was coming to an end. Gradually, the evening sky started to be suffused with the gorgeous crimson glow of the setting sun.

Some wild ducks took off brusquely from the bushes a little distance away. They flew high and joined the sunset clouds that began to gather and float around the horizon.

Suddenly, a lost young duck's heart-wrenching cry shrieked in my head and jolted me out of the imagination of that scene and the thoughts of my father.

The beautiful Athens campus never ceased to enchant.

The university's heart, the lawn outside the College Green, was my favorite spot to sit and dream. Many professors and students seemed to feel the same: they lay, read, chatted, or admired the sky. College Green's brick walkways and shady trees provided a quiet respite to all who sought it.

On the lawn, I encountered some lovely furry creatures – the squirrels – for the first time. Like magic, the cheeky squirrels appeared and vanished around the tree trunks, with which they shared a similar color.

The squirrel's swift movements, big bright eyes, four slim limbs, and cute tiny claws combined with that over-sized tail looked comical and made me laugh aloud whenever I had time to sit and marvel at them.

The Alden Library was another favorite place of mine on campus.

Alden had large windows that let in plenty of sunshine and brought the library's lush green garden views to the students.

I used to sit by a window seat on the fifth floor, having a corner to myself, and spent a whole morning or afternoon there studying, gazing into the space outside.

Campus life was not always rosy, though. It rained a lot during spring.

I had a particular fondness for the rain at night when I was indoors, feeling protected and grateful. But I found it dreadful when it fell on my grocery shopping day on Sunday.

The bus I took to the supermarket would always keep me waiting forever. Sometimes, I walked 40 minutes to the store, shopped, and ventured on another long walk back.

In the usual circumstances, I liked walking. But the walk to and inside the supermarket, and then the walk back with two big bags of heavy groceries to last a week, could be irksome, especially when it rained.

The water puddles and mud on the road added weight to every step and lengthened those tiresome trips.

*

I had been getting As for my papers because I studied hard and researched well for them. It was also because my professors were wise, friendly, and generous with their time.

The professors told us that they held an open-door policy, which meant that we could walk in and speak to them if we found their office doors open and they were there.

I took this thoughtful policy to heart.

Often, I would finish my paper a week before the deadline. Gladly, I walked into my professors' offices and asked them for advice on improving my essay. I would contemplate their comments and make revisions to refine the writing. Then, I submitted my heavily edited article according to the given deadline.

I did this for all four courses I took that semester.

One day, I got a B for a paper in the Practices in Organizational Communication course.

I was shocked at first, then became furious with myself.

Words eluded me.

For a whole day, I floated around empty-headedly.

When I returned to the dormitory that evening, I had no appetite, even though I had not eaten all day.

Study evaded me also.

I sat at my desk all night and could not get anything done.

Finally, I gave up and crawled into my bed.

Sleep escaped me too.

After midnight, when the dormitory quietened down, I found myself creeping back up, opening the door, stepping out, and sliding down by the wall next to the door.

Sitting on the floor, leaning against the wall, I wrapped my hands around my shins and pulled in tight. I lowered my head and started weeping.

Study was the only thing I did well.

It was the only thing to prove my worthiness.

Now, I even failed that.

I heaved and felt my lower backbone push into the wall.

I raged against myself.

In front of my parents, nothing I said had meaning.

To them, my words always seemed insubstantial, facetious, silly, selfish, girlish, bitter, revengeful, irresponsible, unrealistic, unfilial, ungrateful, and troublesome. The synonyms stacked up, rebutting whatever claim I had made, whatever feeling or fact stood behind the assertion, turning my mouth into a black hole.

And then Coach.

The memories of him and his assault continued to render me as nothing.

I shuddered at the thought.

Tightening the wrap around my shins further, I buried my head deeper.

Tears dried, but my mind was in solitary confinement.

I could not find a way out.

A pamphlet appeared on my desk two days afterwards.

On the front page of the pamphlet, it said:

> *While there is life, there is hope.*
> *Ohio University Student Counseling Service*
> *We Are Here For You.*
> *Please call…*

I held the pamphlet and lost my thoughts in it.

When I looked up, I caught a glimpse of my roommate, Sandy.

Sandy was standing in front of her closet and getting ready for class.

A timorous, compassionate smile appeared on her face.

Startled, I wondered if she intended the smile for me.

She looked me in the eye and gave me a definite nod. But just as quickly, she grabbed her jacket and bag and left the room.

A week after the breakdown night, I began seeing a psychologist at the student service center.

The center was bright, simple, and well-organized. There was a square counter with about three staff members at it.

I approached a guy in front. He greeted me and asked me to fill in a short form, which I did. Not long afterward, a man who was probably in his early sixties came out from one of the rooms behind the counter.

The hoary white-haired man was tall, thin, and slightly hunchbacked.

The kindness in his eyes and the wise and quiet air he carried calmed me as he approached.

I knew I had found my safe spot.

A few sessions later, I told my counselor about the sexual assault and the abortion I had experienced. It was my first time revealing these things to anyone. Like a snake shedding its skin, the telling made me feel both aggressive and vulnerable at once.

When I returned to my dormitory and found nobody around, I punched my pillow like a boxer hitting a heavy punchbag. Forcefully, I beat the pad with clenched fists until my upper arms went numb.

But I could not stop. I would not stop.

It felt as if I had to exorcise those crippling memories from my mind and the corroding fits of anger from my body before I stopped. Otherwise, those recollections and rage would turn into bricks and crash through the window of my life one day.

For recovery, I went for long walks.

First, I walked around the bitternut hickory trees in East Green. Then I went further to The Ridges. Some Chinese chestnut and redbud trees surrounded the buildings of The Ridges. I trailed around those trees in hopes of finding some consolation.

Also, I dawdled onto the College Green, wandering around the yellowwoods.

Marching on and on, day after day, I persisted until some peace returned.

The black walnut tree on the west side of the Memorial Auditorium looked secure and protective. I sat underneath it and began dreaming.

In the dream that came, a squirrel ran on the green. My body felt lighter and freer.

But then, my mind would drift back to the past.

After the abortion when I was 20, my menstruation seldom came. Even if it did come every three to six months, it was dark and scarce. The symptom had persisted for years.

Physically, I did not see myself as a woman.

Mentally, I kept thinking I was undeserving of love and unworthy of a devoted lover.

I felt like an alternative, a side dish, if I engaged in a relationship with someone.

And so, I had become involved in short affairs with married men.

A Swiss chef from a reputable five-star hotel had bought me a special-edition Cartier watch. He had especially ordered this watch from the luxury brand's Swiss office with a red watchband to replace its ordinary black one. But whenever I wore it, it felt as if the watch's band ate into my flesh. I lost it soon after.

Sometime later, another high-status professional invited me to travel to Paris with him when he attended conferences. I agreed and tagged along. His Paris hotel room had a spacious balcony directly facing the Eiffel Tower.

The trip happened around the middle of July. On the 14th of that month, the French National Day, the guy took part in an official celebration function.

I stayed alone in the hotel room.

Then, the National Day fireworks started.

I stood on the balcony, leaning on its balustrade, and admired the grandiose fireworks flashing, shooting off right in front of my eyes.

The fireworks' deafening sounds accelerated people's heartbeats and got their adrenaline flowing as they "wowed" and "whoaed" at the top of their lungs.

Then, I realized I was crying.

I cried into the waves of the clamor all around and let it drown out my weeping sounds.

The crowds broke into rapturous applause when the fireworks displayed a grand finale.

I had an impulse to jump into them and bury myself in their laughter.

The affairs, the abrupt burst of tears, and the suicidal thoughts rendered me powerless, voiceless.

I talked about them with my counselor.

He helped me to put the issues into perspective.

For instance, he told me that trauma was not the bad things that happened to me but how I responded to those terrible events. And because I responded by internalizing them, I became disconnected from myself. It was painful to face my weakened and wounded self. Being myself became too vulnerable and scary. But pretending to be someone else took up a lot of energy, hence the chronic fatigue.

Listening to his analysis enabled me to gain alternative viewpoints into my inner self.

I started reorganizing my thoughts and reconstructing my life.

In that safe spot, I felt my strength returning for the first time.

I could loosen the straitjacket of those detrimental dark thoughts and breathe more freely.

*

Ohio University's sister college, Chubu University in Japan, had gifted cherry blossom trees to OU. They represented CU's relationship with OU. During OU's bicentennial, CU made another offer and brought the grove's total to 200 trees.

OU first planted the trees in 1979. Both OU's president Charles Ping and CU's president Kazuo Yamada attended. Then, the cherry tree grove grew, running along the Hocking River between the bike path and Convocation Center.

On the first day of April 2000, when I went for my usual walk toward those cherry tree groves, I raised my head, beholding the cherry blossom buds under a vibrant blue sky.

Maroon tips sprouted and swelled through the sealed bark.

Pigeons ruffled.

The view of the Ridges' buildings provided a majestic backdrop to the budding branches.

When I went by them again a few days later, even the cloudy sky did not look so gloomy with the cherry buds in view.

Another time, raindrops clung to the budding branches, giving them a sheer illusion.

Three days afterward, spring sprang with full blooms around the corner.

Soon enough, white blossoms appeared.

The exquisite flowers emerged into the sparkling sunlight. Their shy, sweet fragrance shrouded me gently.

Then, the trees were all in full bloom in the blink of an eye, and the scent grew bolder, almost intoxicating.

I took my time strolling beneath the beautiful blossoms, inhaling their fragrance, admiring their vivacity, and absorbing their transformative power.

*

And then, I began working out at the fitness room in Ping Center.

Two table-tennis tables stood in the corner between the entrance and the fitness area.

I usually kept my head low and passed those two tables quickly.

One day, I could not help but look over there.

A slim young white man was playing against two others.

The single guy handled the opponents with a sense of ease and grace.

He looked very much like a professional player as he wore proper table tennis attire and held the handshake grip of a fantastic Butterfly brand paddle.

I wanted to challenge him.

So, I walked up to them and waited till they finished the game.

I looked at the slim guy and asked if I could play with him.

He said yes, of course, casually.

He lent me another nice paddle of his.

It suited me well because I was also a handshake grip player.

Furthermore, his paddle was of medium weight, suitable for players like me who played with both attack and defense styles.

I was a stranded whale back in the sea.

When I left the Ping Center that night, it felt like my old friends, Daiyu and Baochai, the protagonists of *Dream of the Red Chamber*, had returned to me.

Daiyu's sensitivity and Baochai's sense cheered me on.

My deep longing to be out there, walk under the night sky, unafraid and beneath the stars, became a reality.

I immersed myself in the serenity around me and the beauty above.

The starry sky turned itself into a heaven-embroidered cloth reflecting golden and silvery lights; the backdrop was blue, dim, and dark all at the same time.

On the ground, cherry blossom petals carpeted the path.

The petals spread under my feet; I tried not to tread on them.

As I skipped joyously along the path, I began softly humming my favorite folk song:

> Don't ask from where I've come
> My hometown is far away
> Why do I wander
> Wander afar.

And then I met Seishi.

Seishi and I took the same course during the spring semester.

He was a sophomore and three years younger than me.

Tall and broad-shouldered, Seishi often wore shorts, flip-flops, and a cap that he pulled low to cover most of his face.

He reminded me of my puppy love from when I was eight and spent most of the summer holiday in my father's hospital playing with the kids there. There was this boy called Ming, who was the only son of the hospital's head.

Ming had three elder sisters. Like Baoyu in *Dream of the Red Chamber*, Ming was the jade of the family, the love of many.

But I did not pay much attention to Ming as I had a close playmate then called Nina.

Nina and I usually wandered freely into the woods and picked up wild berries and flowers as we wished.

One day, Ming came with us. He plucked some white and pink daisies along the trail. I thought he would give them to Nina as I always thought she was the lither and prettier one.

When we reached a brook, Ming suddenly came in front of me.

He handed me the bunch of daisies and ran off.

Seishi and I were the only two Asian students in our class.

He had a girlfriend back in Japan, and I was not ready for a serious relationship. So we did not start dating then, but we certainly clicked.

Seishi appeared to be an introvert at first. As our friendship grew, it was delightful to discover that he was a passionate person full of opinions – an extrovert.

On the other hand, I often acted like an extrovert, a people pleaser, but I was shy and lacked self-confidence.

We became best friends.

Seishi's parents were both chefs, and he inherited their culinary skills.

After school, he often invited me to his dormitory and prepared authentic Japanese dishes such as misoshiru, soba or cold noodles, udon in dashi, beef tataki, and sashimi.

Those dishes he made were indeed ambrosia, the best meals I had had in Athens by far.

After the most satisfying feasts, we would curl up on his couch and chat away blissfully.

Seishi loved to travel and had been an exchange student in Germany, stayed there for a year, and visited most European countries.

I also shared with him my adventures, to which he listened with an open mouth and wide eyes.

In his admiring eyes, I gradually returned to the eight-year-old me: unpretentious and comfortable in my skin.

Seishi and I shared many informative and entertaining evenings.

Mid-June 2000 arrived.

I wore a white daisy dress underneath the black gown for the undergraduate commencement ceremony.

Putting on my square academic cap, I felt its firmness and assured myself that this was my cap and that I was worthy of wearing it.

The soft, champagne gold-colored graduation tassels lightly brushed my cheek.

A sense of happiness lit up my heart and spirit.

I stood before a mirror and stared at this strange, new me.

Suddenly, the past seized the chance and gripped my throat. I shook my head. Taking a deep breath, I held it for one or two seconds and exhaled slowly.

After a few rounds, relief arrived.

The commencement exercise was held indoors in the Convocation Center on the west green of the OU Athens campus. I attended the morning ceremony.

As I entered the center, the brightness of the lighting and the effervescent atmosphere engulfed me.

I stood still at the entrance to let the whole scene register in my mind, making myself believe I had made it this far.

I had arrived.

So many people walked, talked, and laughed all at once inside the center.

I found my seat, settled in, and told myself I belonged.

This service was for me, too.

The OU and American flags were proudly erect on either side of the stage.

It felt like the flags were giving out their blessings.

I leaned back and allowed myself to receive such blessings.

An MC approached the center of the stage and started the ceremony. After the president's speech, there was an honorable guest speaker.

As OU was famous for its journalism major, the university invited a noble graduate who had been a director of speech-writing at the White House and had served three US presidents.

I could neither recall the speaker's name nor take in much of her speech. Still, I was thrilled to be there listening to her.

More importantly, I was very proud of being an imminent Bachelor's degree holder.

It might not have meant as much to the students there with me.

But I knew that I had overcome mountains and seas to get there.

Holding my head high and back straight, I walked up to the stage to receive my diploma.

Like the bottle of achievements that I wished to keep when I was little, I now did obtain something that I could prove to others, but more so to myself:

I was an achiever.

Ever after, in moments of despair, I knew I had something that I could turn to.

That something would always help to remind me:

People could destroy my dreams.

They could never break me.

I will always be the girl who dreamed.

After the ceremony, Seishi, a few other students from Hong Kong, and I decided to celebrate at the restaurant in OU Inn.

When we walked and arrived at that slope where I encountered the Ohio River's view for the first time, I told my friends to go ahead and that I would catch up soon.

Pausing atop that slope, Xu Zhimo's poem, *Chance,* resurfaced. The poem's second and final stanza resonated in my head.

> We meet on the sea on an inky night
> You are on your way; I am on mine
> Remember, if you will
> Or better still, forget
> The light we exude at the moment of our encounter.
> (My translation)

The nights were not so dark and terrifying for me anymore.

The light the OU campus and I exuded during our ephemeral encounter would illuminate the rest of my life. I smiled, immersing myself in this rare, pure moment of happiness.

Another poem by Xu, *Bidding Farewell to Cambridge Again*, also reemerged.

Borrowing his poem's last stanza, I bade my farewell to Ohio University.

> Quietly, I am leaving
> Just as quietly as I came
> Giving a wave with my sleeve
> I don't take away a single cloud.
> (My translation)

Also, I bade farewell to my younger victim self and entered adulthood.

I accepted that I would continue to encounter endless sleepless nights and that anxiety, depression, self-doubts, or worse, self-loathing would always threaten to encroach and suffocate me. But knowing I had found a way forward, I asked myself to travel with hope.

When I began walking toward OU Inn to rejoin my friends, a little blue butterfly flew by, and it seemed to pause right before my eyes.

After an infinitesimal moment, the butterfly's lavender, blue and white gossamer wings took flight, flying into the west wind and leaving behind the sweet, faint scent of renewal.

I took a deep breath, and when I breathed out, I let all the negative experiences leave me. I remembered Coach's face, and I blew it further away. I drew another long breath, brought my arms out in front of me, and spread my fingers.

Fully aware of the physical space I took up in the world, I stretched out my span and raised myself to the early summer sky on my tiptoes. I felt my ribcage expand, and the knots of tension in my neck and shoulders began to loosen and untangle with the welcoming warmth.

Taking a third slow and deliberate breath, I held it and marveled at the wide-open sky that looked like an ocean flat with white surf. Then I exhaled, following the passage of my out-breath through my body.

The 15-year-old me in the plane for the first time, stretching out and admiring the sea of white clouds, came to my mind.

Like my 15-year-old self, I felt clean and complete.

And more than that, I knew I was whole and worthy.

Epilogue

Dear readers, thank you for traveling this far with me. As the book ends when I was 26, I want to bring you up-to-date about me and my family.

My father passed away in 2011 in Sha Tin Hospital, aged only 64. He died of lung cancer. On his death certificate, his occupation is stated as "Building Caretaker." It was his last job after the electronics factory where he had been working for most of his Hong Kong life moved to the mainland.

To me, though, my father, Leung Wailai, would always be a doctor, book lover, and potent introvert who turned his disappointments inward toward his beloved family and, ultimately, toward himself. My dearest flawed father, may you rest in peace.

My mother, in her seventies, apart from having latent illnesses, is well. She walks and stretches every early morning for two hours. Then, she takes care of the housework and looks after my elder sister's two children as she lives with them in Ma On Shan.

Elder Brother lives with his own family nearby. He visits Mother and has breakfast, lunch, or dinner there whenever possible. It is an open secret that he loves Mother's cooking more than his wife's.

His wife, my only sister-in-law, is hospitable. Our family gatherings mainly take place at their house these days.

Younger Sister and I are friends. Elder Sister and I are friends. Frictions between the two that developed when I was away need resolving. Younger Sister and I are working on it. We try not to let Elder Sister retreat into herself like our father did.

Elder Sister, Elder Brother, and Younger Sister have grown children. Mother feels okay with me remaining single and without children. She cherishes my reconnection with the family.

Yes, Mother, your *Ling-er* ["child" in Hokkien] will be okay.

To me, my mother, Chan Wingwai, will always be a teacher, patriot, and responsible mother.

I will be 50 by the time this book is published in 2024. With joy, I report that the girl who dreamed exists exuberantly in me as I continue to create art and speak my truth.

Like Cao Xueqin and his *Dream of the Red Chamber*, it has taken me ten years to write and find a publisher for this memoir.

Cao's book inspired me to dream. Therefore, I would like to close with my translation of his words at the beginning of *Dream*.

Absurd words occupy these pages,
capturing my tears over the years.
Everyone considers the author mad,
but who understands what it is like?

Author's Acknowledgments

I thank
Adeline Huang, my friend and family,
Mark Schipp, my friend and first reader, the backbone of my writing,
Xu Xi, Ira Sukrungruang, and Susanne Antonetta, my MFA mentors,
Pete Spurrier, the publisher of my memoir.
Without you, this book would not exist –
my dream would not come true.
Thank you.

EXPLORE ASIA WITH BLACKSMITH BOOKS

From booksellers around the world or from *www.blacksmithbooks.com*